Among Generations
The Cycle of Adult Relationships

D0145338

Among Generations
The Cycle of Adult Relationships

Joan E. Norris, Ph.D., and Joseph A. Tindale, Ph.D.
Department of Family Studies
University of Guelph
Guelph, Ontario

W. H. Freeman and Company
NEW YORK

Library of Congress Cataloging-in-Publication Data

Norris, Joan E.
Among generations : the cycle of adult relationships / by Joan E. Norris and
Joseph A. Tindale.
        p.   cm.
    Includes bibliographical references and index.
    ISBN 0-7167-2206-2. — ISBN 0-7167-2207-0 (pbk.)
    1. Parent and adult child—United States.   2. Intergenerational
relations—United States.   3. Life cycle, Human. I. Tindale,
Joseph Arthur, 1948-   . II. Title.
HQ755.86.N67 1993
306.874—dc20

                                                                93-5972
                                                                CIP

Copyright © 1994 by W. H. Freeman and Company

PRINTED IN THE UNITED STATES OF AMERICA

1 2 3 4 5 6 7 8 9 0   VB   9 9 8 7 6 5 4 3

For our families, who inspired us to ask the questions raised in this book and provided the support we needed to answer them.

Contents

Preface

Some years ago, we and our group of friends were starting families and purchasing homes for the first time. We noticed, with surprise and some chagrin, that all of us had been helped by our parents to establish independent households. Often the help was financial, but frequently it involved advice and labor as well. We knew that much of the gerontology literature from the scientific community took the position that support flowed from young to old, but our observations suggested that often help was provided by older parents to their adult children. These observations prompted questions about helping each other "among generations." We wondered how, how often, and with what social psychological consequences such support came about within multigenerational families. We also wondered whether it was repaid and, if so, how?

When we delved further into the research literature on the family for answers to these questions, we noticed significant gaps. Researchers had rarely considered how families change and adapt across the life course, and they had not often considered how the married couple weathers these changes. In particular, there was very little discussion of the kind and amount of support exchanged over the intergenerational life span between parents and their children. Scientific studies of the relations between members of the parental couple, and between the couple and siblings and friends, neglected to consider the nature of long-term exchanges of support. In 1989, two prominent family researchers, Jay Mancini and Rosemary Blieszner, argued that "the family must be analyzed as a system of interdependent lives, and socialization must be recognized as a reciprocal, lifelong process." Clearly this recommendation has not received sufficient attention.

Just as clearly, variations in exchanges of support because of variations in family composition (e.g., single-parent households), ethnicity, or social class have not been examined systematically. There is some research available on ethnic differences in the structure and support of young families (Mindel & Habenstein, 1981). Gerontology research on older members of ethnic minorities in the United States, however, has only been done recently. African-Americans did not receive much consideration in research before the 1960s, Hispanics were not made the focus of study until the 1970s, and it was only in the 1980s that increased attention was paid to Asian-Americans, aboriginals, and Americans of European descent (Markides, Liang, & Jackson, 1990). Nevertheless, when it comes to studies of intergenerational relations in later life that also have an orientation to ethnic and class variability, the scientific literature still is woefully undeveloped. Unfortunately, recent research does not show much promise of improvement. An analysis of six prominent psychology journals demonstrated that research on African-Americans is becoming less, rather than more, prevalent (Graham, 1992).

Among Generations: The Cycle of Adult Relationships was written to address limitations in existing research on families in later life. Our goal was to consider the perspective of both members of a married couple throughout their lives as they create and participate in intergenerational relations with family and friends. The question guiding us was How do couples become involved in intergenerational relations and with what results?

We took this general question and applied it to specific circumstances. For example, in our opening anecdote we describe the experience of one of our parents in providing support for the other generations in his family. We then explore the continuing negotiation among the generations that accompanies such support. Our exploration of issues like this required us to delve into other dimensions of the parental couple's support system. In this way, we found it absolutely necessary to consider peer relations with siblings and with friends when considering what meanings emerge within intergenerational exchanges.

Relationships among generations have been considered within two conceptual frameworks, attachment and reciprocity. "Attachment" refers to the close emotional bond that family members typically share. "Reciprocity" describes the efforts family members make to balance their giving and taking across the course of their lives. In *Among Generations* we have argued that parents engage in the exchange of support with their children and that these exchanges change and mature along with the individuals involved. We make the point that attachment is the emotional cement that maintains the supportive framework of family relations when cracks appear in the relational brickwork. The stress leading to cracks may be caused by decisions regarding short-term exchanges involving practically all family members, e.g., what will be done with the family cottage? Stress may also result from very particular exchanges between members of the family: for example, under what circumstances does a parent post bond for a child who has been in trouble before? In each case, the family normally withstands the stresses of everyday life because attachment facilitates long-term sensitivity to issues of fairness, equity, and reciprocity.

In dealing with a variety of later-life family issues, differentiated by culture and a range of socioeconomic conditions, we have mined the literature and our own data as creatively as possible. In some cases we have discussed research that was not originally presented within an intergenerational family context. We have noted how this work can inform the questions that this book addresses and offered our own conclusions. For example, the literature on friendship discussed in Chapter 6 focuses on the individual at one age, and often under one set of circumstances. We have taken this work and suggested a perspective that involves the developing couple. Wherever possible, we have also noted how differences in family structure and cultural or ethnic background within a North American context might influence the course of the couple's relations with friends.

The book is structured to engage the reader in the story of a maturing couple. We begin our examination with the process whereby two individuals make a decision to become a couple. We then consider the implications that follow from their decision to become parents, as well as the intergenerational relations that result from this decision. Throughout this process we have examined the variable circumstances in which such family processes may be experienced.

Writing this book clarified, for us, the processes involved in the exchange of support within multigenerational families. Our analyses support the view that parents' offers of help to adult children are not isolated and unusual events. Rather, they are part of the ongoing, mutual give-and-take that occurs and is mediated by the attachment bonds of love and respect.

In considering the complexity of these intergenerational family relations we received important feedback from several people. Our senior editors at Freeman, originally Jonathan Cobb and later Susan Brennan, both made a vital and constructive contribution in integrating the feedback we received from several reviewers, Victor G. Cicirelli, Purdue University; Vern L. Bengtson, University of Southern California; Sarah H. Matthews, Cleveland State University; Jay A. Mancini, Virginia Polytechnic Institute and State University; and Helena Znaniecka Lopata, Loyola University of Chicago. We are also grateful to our project editor, Janet Tannenbaum, for guiding us through the often bewildering process of copyediting as painlessly as possible. Others who receive our thanks for reading chapters at our request include several colleagues at the University of Guelph—Gerald Adams and Susan Lollis, Department of Family Studies; and Monique Gignac, Gerontology Research Centre—as well as colleagues from further afield: James Gladstone, Department of Social Work, McMaster University; Sarah Matthews, Department of Sociology, Cleveland State University; and Iteka Weeda, Wageningen Agricultural University, Netherlands. Our gratitude is also extended to the Social Sciences and Humanities Research Council of Canada for support they extended to the research projects we cited in reporting our data.

Among Generations
The Cycle of Adult Relationships

Couple Maturation in an Intergenerational Context

In 1930, when he was 12 years old, Joan Norris's father, Poul, together with his sister, Else, and his parents, Oldi and Kristian, emigrated from Denmark to Canada. Kristian worked as a laborer in a small-town factory, and Poul worked during the summer in the tobacco fields to help make ends meet in the family. Later, after leaving high school, spending five years overseas during World War II, and working in a bank, Poul was able to save enough to help Oldi and Kristian purchase a house.

This pattern of intergenerational support was maintained in Poul's family as he grew older, married, and raised three children of his own. In his early retirement years, he was still providing care for Kristian, who was then in his 90s and had been widowed for over 30 years, as well as helping launch his own children. After helping to pay for their post-secondary education, Poul found himself helping with the downpayment and mortgages on his children's houses. At one point during the years of his children's young adulthood, as they were establishing their own families, he pointed out that he had investment in five properties belonging to three generations.

The Dynamics of Intergenerational Relations

The intergenerational support captured in this anecdote about Joan's family can be found in many variations in different family situations. This

family is Western European, but the family might be of any other ethnicity, or combination of ethnicities via marriage. Similarly, when parents
and adult children ask their family for mortgage relief or help with a
downpayment, economic times might be good or bad.

It must also be acknowledged, therefore, that the historical context
has an impact on the kind of support exchanged within families, and
indeed whether help is provided at all. In our example, Poul's parents
found themselves in need after weathering the Great Depression with
few financial resources. His children, on the other hand, found themselves attempting to purchase a home during a time of inflated prices that
came about after the housing market boomed through the late 1980s,
when interest rates and unemployment levels were low. A few years ago,
in a series of Canadian magazine articles (Fennel, Luckow, Daly, &
Jenish, 1988), the authors described how runaway housing prices were
placing most prospective first-time homeowners in a bind. They could
not buy a house without either winning a lottery or getting what Joan's
husband, Randy, refers to as G.I. (good-in-law) financing.

More recently, young couples seeking to buy a house or trying to pay
the mortgage have faced recession economics and the prospect of losing
money on their investment ("negative equity"; Dolen, 1992). And while
parents are a potential source of help, they too are economically vulnerable—to job loss, low returns on retirement savings plans, and reduction in retirement income.

Intergenerational support also takes the form of parents' allowing
adult children to return home to live for either a short or relatively
extended period of time. This kind of support and the ongoing negotiation of reciprocity and attachment relations associated with it are the
core of this book. The term reciprocity has its roots in exchange theory,
which traditionally has been focused on single exchanges, even as they
occur within ongoing relationships. The concept of global reciprocity,
however, refers to the long-term balancing of a series of single exchanges. These exchanges typically take place within close relationships,
i.e., attachments, and may appear in any specific situation to be im-
balanced or inequitable. Over the life cycle of a family, though, balance is
likely to be achieved.

The phenomenon of incompletely launched children is fully discussed in Chapter 3; our purpose at this point is to note its occurrence
and place it in historical and cultural context. Between 1953 and 1974 the
proportion of Americans aged 20–24 who lived with their parents

Reprinted with special permission of King Features Syndicate.

dropped significantly. For males, it decreased from 53.4% to 40.5%, and for females, from 35% to 26.1% (Schnaiberg & Goldenberg, 1989, p. 254). Since then, however, the proportion has increased, especially for men. In the period 1974 to 1988, for males it went from 40.5% to 50.7%, almost a return to the 1953 levels. Women saw their proportion climb from 26.1% to 33.6% (Schnaiberg & Goldenberg, 1989, p. 254; Glick & Lin, 1986; Clemens & Axelson, 1985).

A similar phenomenon has been observed in Canada. Census data for single males and females between the ages of 20 and 29 in the period 1971 to 1986 were analyzed by Boyd and Pryor (1989). Between 1971 and 1976 the levels of young adults residing with their parents were steady or increasing slightly. Between 1981 and 1986, however, the levels increased more substantially. For females, it increased from 25.8% to 31.1%, and for males, from 31.2% to 34.8%. The population of Canadians 20 to 29 years of age who lived at home in 1981 could be characterized as having low income, a Mediterranean mother tongue, a high school education or less, and not being in the labor force (Boyd & Pryor, 1989, pp. 474–475).

There are several possible explanations for the increase in the proportion of young adults living with their parents. One is that these people are lacking maturity; another cites surplus labor in times of stagnant economies (Schnaiberg & Goldenberg, 1989; Glick & Lin, 1986; Clemens & Axelson, 1985).

The question Boyd and Pryor (1989) see looming large for future research is, What are the effects of children living at home on the relationship between them and their parents? When children either return home or do not leave until sometime well into their 20s, their parents incur increased household expenses and also lose some of their privacy. In one study, researchers interviewed 29 couples who were extending aid to children who had grown, left home, and then returned for assistance because of problems like divorce, chemical dependency, and unemployment (Greenberg & Becker, 1988). The results suggest that parents were an important source of support for children experiencing difficulty. Providing this support, however, takes a financial and emotional toll on parents and may make children more dependent, especially if the "good-in-law" financiers feel they have the right to oversee all the children's significant spending.

These problems may result in parent–child and intracouple conflict (Schnaiberg & Goldenberg, 1989; Clemens & Axelson, 1985; Boyd & Pryor, 1989). However difficult such circumstances may be though, Glick and Lin (1986) maintain that both generations are consoled by the knowledge that the shared roof is temporary and is preferable to the alternatives. But as circumstances change, the alternatives may begin to look better. The suitability of the temporary arrangements is something that both generations continually reassess. These reassessments, in which family members in each generation must analyze their respective stakes in the short and long term, are part of a lifelong exchange whose overall objective is equity.

Despite parental efforts in supporting their adult children, the gerontological literature is dominated by a view of older parents as frail and in need of care by children. A survey of several years of research among the major American gerontological journals found that the overwhelming majority of articles on caregiving were focused on the level of burden carried by children (Greenberg & Becker, 1988). While some social scientists (e.g., Connidis, 1989b) recognize that many parents care for adult children, research literature on this subject is almost nonexistent.

The assumption that one generation may be unfairly advantaged relative to another does not serve either one very well (Kingson, Hirshorn, & Cornman, 1986). Although both generations make sacrifices when parents extend support, each generation is also rewarded. The young couple receive tangible and intangible support, and the parents have the satisfaction of having helped out their children (even if they would just as soon not be needed quite so much). These rewards are "ties that bind" (Kingson, Hirshorn, & Cornman, 1986), a phrase used as the title of a monograph sponsored by the Gerontological Society of America; the thesis of this work is that intergenerational relations are characterized more by mutual interdependence and reciprocity than by conflict. This approach is likely an accurate reflection of the character of family relations across the life span: Generally, parents want to help their children, even when it necessitates sacrifice, and children seek help only when they truly need it, and yearn for the day when they can be more independent.

At the same time, intergenerational conflict may be inevitable when events make one generation appear advantaged relative to others. Certain social policies, such as tax relief for mortgage payments, have different effects on different generations. These effects are determined by circumstances of people in each generation when they are young and need to obtain a mortgage. For example, Americans (unlike Canadians) benefit from being able to claim mortgage interest as a tax deduction. The generation of parents who purchased homes many years prior to the introduction of this tax break is disadvantaged relative to adult children making home purchases after its introduction. Intergenerational conflict is exacerbated when people forget that times really were different when the parents sought their first mortgage. This is true regardless of which generation had an easier time of it.

Conceptualizing Intergenerational Family Relations

Attachment in Parent–Child Relations

Attachment theory was developed to explain the strong bond that mothers and infants normally establish with one another (e.g., Bowlby, 1969). Researchers in the field of child development view secure attachment as the product of an ongoing well-functioning relationship between parent and child. These researchers have produced evidence to support a link between secure attachments in early childhood and healthy peer and family relationships in later childhood (LaFreniere & Sroufe, 1985). Young children becoming "securely attached" (Bowlby, 1969) to their parents is a good predictor of adolescent adjustment. Similarly, adolescent attachment to family and friends predicts midlife adjustment (Tesch, 1989). Adjustment reflects a view held by children that their relationship with their parents is supportive, characterized by affection, and, on the whole, equitable.

Until recently, researchers have not attempted to extend the attachment perspective to parent–child relationships during adulthood. Instead, researchers studying such relationships have merely provided descriptions of observed phenomena, in the absence of a theoretical framework. The largest body of research in this vein deals with the effects of caregiving on adult children and their frail parents (e.g., Brody, Hoffman, Kleban, & Schoonover, 1989). Such descriptive studies lack explanatory power. For example, it is difficult to understand why providing support for a parent is perceived as burdensome by one daughter but not by her sister, who actually provides more support. A study using an attachment framework that considers the history of the bonds between daughters and the parent may shed some light on these differences. As researchers on sibling relationships have pointed out recently, brothers and sisters may have markedly different "nonshared environments" within the same family, based on the strength of their attachment to their parents and to each other (e.g., Dunn & Plomin, 1991).

While the attachment perspective is useful in explaining why older parents and their children have an emotional stake in maintaining harmonious family interactions, both sides have different experiences of attachment. Children feel an emotional attachment to their parents that is derived from their initial physical dependence on them (Bowlby, 1980). As the children grow into middle childhood, a sense of emotional closeness between parent and child develops, persists, and matures (Troll & Smith, 1976). During the teenage years, children begin to experience a need for separateness from their parents. At that point, attachment bonds are likely to be less intense as the adolescent explores relationships with peers, and parents look forward to an emptying nest (Cooper, Grotevant, & Condon, 1983). Eventually, attachment feelings become feelings of protectiveness as parents themselves become physically dependent (Cicirelli, 1991a). Aging parents, on the other hand, typically feel less attachment to their active parenting roles (Norris, 1987a). Instead, their commitment appears to be to the continuity of the family as a whole.

The concept of attachment is relevant to a discussion of conflict and equity in parent–child relations across the life span. For example, parents' experience of attachment is affected by children returning home to "refill the nest" (Mancini & Blieszner, 1989). If, as we think, attachment to one's children is developmental, then it is unlikely that attachment levels would increase when son or daughter returns to the nest, suitcase in hand, child in tow. A more likely scenario is that the positive feelings associated with attachment would further decline because of the inevitable disruptions of having a child move back home.

The literature has identified a range of coherent and linked characteristics of the attachment of children to family and friends. First among these is the need for proximity to the principal attachment figure in times of stress. Joseph's nine-year-old daughter recently made it quite clear that if she were going to the dentist, she wanted her mother, and not her father, to accompany her. In an effort to let her father down gently, she told Joe he was the "coolest dad on the street" but she would be more comfortable in that difficult situation with mom. Similarly, children are comfortable when with a parent and uneasy or anxious when the parent is inaccessible (Weiss, 1982). When, for example, preschool children become separated from the parent in a grocery store, they quickly lose their sense of security and ability to deal with this public place.

After childhood, attachment relations evolve to include the characteristics of durability (Bowlby, 1973) and mutuality (West, Sheldon, & Reiffer, 1987). As adolescents become more independent, they are able to appreciate that their relationships will endure beyond lengthy absences when they leave home to find work or attend school. Attachment becomes more clearly an emotional closeness that transcends physical immediacy. This sense of the durability of relationships also allows adults to experience mutuality, i.e., to feel comfortable supporting one another over the long term. In young adulthood, then, children who are attached to their parents realize that while they may have temporary conflicts with them—over inequities in the relationship or differences in outlook—the attachment is not threatened.

Thus, it can be seen that part of the maturation process involves shifting one's attachment from a physical to an emotional and symbolic sphere. Identification with parents is the means whereby children manifest symbolic attachment. This attachment is expressed in their affection for their parents (Cicirelli, 1983b; Cicirelli, 1991; Shaver & Hazan, 1988; Hazan & Shaver, 1987). It also appears to transcend ethnic and cultural boundaries. Symbolic attachment between parent and child has been supported where tested in ethnic minority populations (e.g., Bond, Harvey, & Greenwood, 1991, in a study of Mennonite families in Canada).

Children's original attachment to their parents continues and develops concurrent with their becoming attached to others. When parents are older and in failing health, children respond to this threat to attachment by helping them in a process that reflects a life-span conception of reciprocity. Interaction with parents, however, can also be prompted by feelings of filial obligation. The nature of the parent–child relationship and the stress of caregiving can lead to conflicts that result in negative feelings co-existing with the positive dimensions of attachment.

Cicirelli (1983b) sought to explore the role of attachment when adult children help their parents. He was interested in finding out whether children care for their parents only out of filial obligation, i.e., a sense of duty—as many gerontologists have suggested—or whether emotional bonds also play an important role. He found that attachment feelings did promote caregiving by adult children. He also found that only when feelings of obligation were accompanied by feelings of attachment did children report that they would help a parent in need. A sense of duty was insufficient reason on it own. Further, the extent of parental dependency made a difference in the helping behavior of children. Most interestingly, his results suggest that appealing directly to filial obligation to encourage children to take on caregiving roles is not effective. Fostering attachment might well prove more productive in encouraging children to provide help to ailing parents.

A study by Thompson and Walker (1984) supports this contention and suggests that the process works for both children and their parents. Reciprocated helping seems more likely when both feel emotionally close. Thompson and Walker examined the interaction of exchange and attachment in mother–daughter pairs. They found that when there were high levels of mutually felt attachment, both were likely to report perceived reciprocity in their helping relations. If the strength of attachment feelings differed between a mother and daughter, however, reciprocity in their exchanges of help was seen as low.

Attachment of children to their parents becomes more complex when there are siblings involved. Adult children caring for frail parents face loss of a source of attachment when parents die. Not surprisingly, then, siblings tend to grow closer as they age and share in the caregiving of their parents. Part of this process involves righting old wrongs among the siblings (Cicirelli, 1989). The supposition is that there is increased motivation to resolve old difficulties and those that arise from the stress of caregiving. When adult children lose their parents, the attachment to siblings further intensifies.

Cicirelli (1989) hypothesized that parental well-being would be improved if the attachment between siblings were strong, and if sisters were involved. A close bond between sisters was associated with parental well-being, but attachment between brothers had no effect. Cicirelli (1989) speculates that if sisters are not on good terms, the parents run a greater risk of being left without caregivers than if this were the case with brothers. He is probably quite right. Another study found that female siblings who were not principal caregivers were uncomfortable in their secondary status, while the same could not be said for brothers (Brody et al., 1989).

Reciprocity Across the Life Span

The sharing of resources within families typically has been considered from the perspective of exchange theory (e.g., Dowd, 1975; Dowd, 1980). Exchange theory rests on an assumption that a relationship will be most satisfying when an act of exchange is reciprocal. Equity theorists (Walster, Walster, & Berscheid, 1978) take this a step further and postulate that a relationship will be most satisfying when a reciprocal exchange is also balanced. Exchange theory is limited by its mechanistic assumption that individuals, when in interaction with others, are motivated to maximize social rewards and minimize costs. The context of the exchange, and the history of the relationship, may be ignored entirely. Take, for instance, the hypothetical case of a mother who allowed a newly divorced adult daughter and her offspring to move back home: According to exchange theory, the mother would expect immediate restitution, perhaps in the form of household labor, to preserve good parent–child interactions.

One empirical study suggests, however, that, at least if she were elderly, the mother might well have no such expectation. In a study of 302 fathers and mothers ranging in age from 65 to 97, McCullough (1990) found little evidence to support either exchange or equity theory. McCullough notes that "older adults may not expect their intergenerational exchanges to be even at one point in time" (McCullough, 1990, p. S154). Instead, they anticipate reciprocity over the long term, i.e., global reciprocity.

Global reciprocity can best be understood from a life-span developmental perspective on the family (Lewis, 1990; Norris, 1987b; Norris & Rubin, 1984). Within this framework, development is seen as continuous and not broken into discrete stages that require crisis resolution to transcend. Unlike more traditional developmental approaches, life-span developmental theory has moved beyond the view that development is driven only by biology, a view that associated social development only with physical development. Baltes and his colleagues (e.g., Baltes, Reese, & Lipset, 1980) have argued persuasively that in development a strong interaction exists between biological and social factors. Thus, recent research has focused on the social experience of aging as people live through various kinds of life events. These include normative events typical of a certain chronological age (child bearing or menopause), as well as experiences associated with historical influences (economic recession or war). They also include nonnormative, or unusual, events (death of a child or winning of a lottery).

Individual adaptation to events such as these occurs within the context of interdependent family relationships. These relationships sustain and constrain people as they negotiate their environment. Shifting patterns of interdependencies are likely as family members continue to grow and develop. By focusing on the family's role in this growth, we can identify the circumstances and times when the balance of interdependence shifts (Lewis, 1990).

One example of this, a situation that we address in more detail in Chapter 4, occurs when a couple's teenage daughter becomes pregnant without any planning for parenthood and the ongoing support of a partner. When this occurs, the parents must make some kind of adaptation to their impending role transitions. They argue, both in their heads and in social interactions, with their daughter, who has challenged their understood reality. In the minds of the parents the information confronts all of their experience; in their interpersonal exchanges they test which interpretation of the new reality finds support in the context of significant relationships, including their marriage. This social flexibility, and sometimes the lack of it, has encouraged theorists to think in terms of the "plasticity" of behavior (Norris, 1987b).

Equity in Parent–Child Relations

A change in a family relationship necessarily destabilizes it. People then reconsider whether their exchanges within that relationship are just or equitable. In making this evaluation, they assess "who is entitled to what from whom" (Lerner, 1981).

The history of the relationship plays a major role in determining the outcome of this assessment of entitlement. Lerner's (1981) conceptualization of the interrelationship of emotional closeness and perceived justice is helpful in understanding these perceptions. This framework describes relationships as "identity," "unit," or "nonunit," based on shared characteristics. When family members feel that they have similar interests, beliefs, and feelings, they are in an identity relationship. This sense of sharing and emotional closeness then creates a perception that their support for one another is mutual and fair. Any transgressions away from equity by individual members are likely to be seen as temporary and forgivable. If, however, family members feel that they have similar interests but lack emotional closeness, they are in a unit relationship and thus less likely to see their support for one another as equitable. Resentment may build if a family member shows a lapse in his or her contributions to the fund of support. One further situation is possible: members who share little and do not feel close to one another are said to be in a nonunit relationship. Each member's contributions are perceived as being inequitable, but this situation is regarded as understandable, given the lack of shared perceptions of the relationship.

We can apply Lerner's conceptualization to predict that parents who want to give assistance to a child without requiring anything tangible in return are not likely to create hard feelings either between themselves and the child, or between themselves and their other children. The family members are in an identity relationship; they identify with each other in this time of need and do not expect balance among everyone (Lerner, Somers, Reid, & Tierney, 1988).

These identity relations are probably also supported by the developmental stage of older parents. There is evidence that helping behavior, driven by altruism, is developmentally appropriate (Kahana, Midlarsky, & Kahana, 1987). This means that an older parent providing assistance to an adult child may feel that the child is entitled to help and that the relationship is just, even if reciprocation from the child is low. The implication is that the parent is looking at the relationship in its entirety rather than at entitlement in the near term.

When family members are not in an identity relationship and attachment levels are not mutual, they may not have this long-term view of familial reciprocity. In families such as these, some members may seek balance in social support given and received on a short-term basis, perhaps even in each situation.

Families with stable identity relations are able to sustain challenges to given understandings of social support; families without such relations are not. This is consistent with the global reciprocity that prevails in the ongoing developmental attachment characterizing most parent–child relations (Antonucci, 1976; Troll & Smith, 1976; Cicirelli, 1983a; Mancini & Blieszner, 1989).

In one family characterized by long-term identity relations, Margaret, Joseph's sister, went to stay with their mother, Rachel, after the birth of her first baby because she and her husband, Wayne, had miscalculated how long it would take to renovate their century-old home. When the baby arrived, they were still up to their necks in dust and without a functional bathroom. All of Margaret's siblings recognized her need and accepted their mother's assistance, thinking it would also give Rachel company in her adjustment to the recent loss of her second husband.

The relationship became strained when the stay, which was initially expected to last only four weeks, stretched to four months. By this time Margaret's mother wanted to begin living independently as a widow, and the rest of the children worried about the strain on her of providing sustained caregiving.

From here the situation could have developed in either of two ways: The identity relationship could have given way to a unit relationship in which all individuals involved consciously sought to redress an imbalance in support. If a solution were not found, resentment was likely from all family members. Alternatively, if there were a perception that justice was being violated consistently, then a remote nonunit relationship could have emerged. In the view of Lerner et al. (1988), strains that emerge in a related situation—when siblings care for ailing parents—result in the breakdown from identity to either unit or nonunit relations. Lerner et al. (1988) feel that the departure from identity relations may persist over the long term. We believe that, given healthy attachment relations among family members, this is not likely; positive identity relationships should be maintained or reemerge once the caregiving crisis has passed.

As it turned out, a unit relationship did emerge, but only briefly. The discomfort felt between mother and daughter was aired, and Margaret urged Wayne to very quickly complete the renovations necessary to permit her and the baby to move back home. As soon as the issue was resolved, the stability inherent in the identity relation was quickly reestablished. Because its members were able to communicate difficulties and seek solutions, the family never deteriorated to the point of manifesting nonunit relations.

This is not to say that in every case the deterioration of intergenerational identity relations is necessarily resolved and identity relations reasserted. It is to say, however, that normally, long-term familial identity relations are strong enough that attachment will override a short-term upset in understandings of what is equitable. Even a severe upset can be resolved, and identity relations reestablished, if it does not seriously violate the underlying foundation of attachment.

To summarize, in adult attachment relations the need for proximity is expressed overwhelmingly in symbolic terms until declining health by the parent or a return home by the child reestablishes some physical proximity. While caregiving for parents may be motivated by filial obligation, a much stronger incentive is attachment, expressed as affection. Reciprocity in parent–child relations is also associated with attachment, and the same appears to be true for reciprocity between siblings, especially sisters. Lifelong attachment between parents and children, and between siblings, provides an incentive for global reciprocity to prevail over short-term inequities and breakdowns of identity relations to unit or nonunit relations.

Our conceptual framework integrates exchange relations, expressed in terms of equity and reciprocity, with attachment relations, expressed in terms of emotional closeness. For our purposes, exchanges involve couples, parents and children, siblings, and friends. Throughout these relations reciprocity and attachment are established within a life-span context. Though temporary conflicts may occur, an overall sense of reciprocity and enduring attachment typically reestablishes the identity relations that those involved depend on for their well-being.

Applying the Framework

In this chapter, we have introduced a conceptual framework: the understanding of attachment and its role in mediating long-term equity and reciprocity in intergenerational relations. By contrast, the chapters that follow are principally substantive.

We begin in Chapter 2 with the couple when they are making decisions about taking out mortgages and becoming parents. Chapter 3 takes the couple through to the point of "launching" the children. In Chapter 4 we ask what grandparents add to the negotiated reciprocity of intergenerational relations. In Chapter 5, we approach the study of relations between siblings the same way we approach the study of friendship.

In what ways do adult siblings strengthen or weaken intergenerational relations in the family? Chapter 6 considers the development and maintenance of reciprocity in attachment relations between friends. Chapter 7, the conclusion, suggests avenues for future research and practice that can facilitate a spirited give-and-take in life-span attachment relations.

Throughout the book we interweave examples of how the rich tapestry of cultural variations and differing economic circumstances creates different expressions of attachment and reciprocity relations which can still be held together by one theoretical thread.

In each chapter the conceptual framework of attachment is applied to the substantive content, integrating our arguments. In Chapter 6, for example, we discuss how the development and maintenance of friendships is built on an understanding of long-term reciprocity and an ongoing mature attachment between nonfamily members. While relations between friends have a value in their own right, our primary interest is in how they provide support to older couples undergoing changes in relations with their children.

We began this book with a portrait of Poul, an important provider of support to multiple generations. Using the theoretical perspectives introduced in this chapter, we can now see how the strong bonds of attachment he shared with his parents and children predicted that Poul would help them when he could. Our analysis also suggests that, in such situations, immediate restitution is not likely. Instead, close families operate on principles of global reciprocity, a sense that whatever they contribute is balanced over the course of their lives by what they receive. Tangible and intangible commodities are exchanged freely throughout that time, and no one keeps a precise score.

It is important to remember that people like Poul are also part of wider networks of social relationships outside their immediate families. The chapters that follow this one will discuss the carefully orchestrated exchanges of support in which all of us take part. We will see that attachment in each specific relationship has a significant impact on expectations for exchange.

Developing Partners

Joan Norris's father likes to tell his friends that he became a grandfather before his children became parents. This situation came about because the Norrises became parents through the adoption of their daughter, Sarah. The story goes that ten years ago, on the day before Christmas, their social worker tried to contact Joan and her husband, Randy, to tell them that they had been selected as the adoptive parents of a baby girl. At the time of the call, however, they were traveling to their parents' homes for the holiday. The social worker then called ahead to Joan's father to tell him the news, which he, in turn, gave to his daughter and son-in-law when they arrived.

The Norrises' transition to parenthood was unusual in that it telescoped into a few days many of the physical and psychological preparations that couples make for a new baby. Nevertheless, the transition was also typical because of the challenges produced to the couple's relationship: the need for communication and the modification of marital roles. In addition, their transition was facilitated by both Joan's and Randy's parents. Like many couples who become "on-time" grandparents, i.e., when they expect to and when social norms support their new identity, they threw themselves into their new role with enthusiasm.

This enthusiasm manifested itself in a wide variety of supports for the new parents. The grandparents helped with the selection and purchasing of the necessary baby supplies. Later, they provided financial support to enable Joan and Randy to purchase a new house. As one friend remarked, "Babies are good for parent–child relationships as well as the economy!"

This chapter examines the dynamics of individual development in the early years of a young couple's marriage. Development is considered in terms of the couple's interaction with each other, their children, parents, and friends. The focus will be on the processes that carry young marrieds forward as they take on new roles. The successful transition to parenthood, for example, can be seen as resulting from ongoing role negotiations between husband and wife in the context of social factors (e.g., the dual career marriage, culture, finances), biological factors (e.g., parental age, childbearing experience), and family life cycle factors (e.g., changing patterns of support from children, the extended family, and friends). Our treatment of such processes is brief, as we intend not to provide an exhaustive discussion of them, but rather to place them in the context of the overall family life cycle relations the couple is experiencing.

As we explained in the first chapter, people who are firmly attached to each other as partners in a couple, in parent–child interaction, as siblings, or as friends, do not expect discrete reciprocity in any specific situation. Instead, these people expect that the overall length and breadth of their relationships will be characterized by a global reciprocity. Even when emotionally close identity relations are in a period of strain, the participants know what boundaries on behavior will fit within the relationship over the long term, if not at that particular moment. In the case of developing partners, members of a couple are embarking on an evolving set of relationships with each other. As they move forward in their new family life cycle, significant changes are typically marked by transition points, as with the transition to parenthood.

The relationships within the couple are the base for a succeeding network of associations. With or without children, the couple will have relations with respective in-laws. Where there are children, the couple become parents and the in-laws become grandparents. Similarly, the children are individuals, daughters or sons, grandchildren and, where there is more than one child, siblings.

Throughout this process all concerned will build, and constantly revise, a set of expectations that allow for ups and downs in relationships provided that the overall expectations of reciprocity appear viable. Obviously, some couple relationships do not respect this global reciprocity, and they often suffer strain when expectations of reciprocity become more explicit and short-term. Nevertheless, when these relationships collapse, new family structures result. Single-parent and step-parent family units move back toward establishing the bases for long-term understandings of what can be expected. The dialectics of reciprocity are ongoing in initial marriages and any reformations of these families.

The Social Context of Marriage

The maturation of attachment begins when two people form an ongoing couple relationship, and must be understood in a social context extending beyond the dyad. The institution of marriage has changed greatly over time. As shown in the table on page 18, the trend in birth cohorts until the 1930s was for marriage and birth of first child to occur at progressively younger ages. The birth cohort of the 1930s became the mothers of the baby boom. Since that time, the trend has been for age at marriage and birth of first child to increase. In the last 20 years, divorce rates have also increased in North America, particularly in the United States (Gee & Kimball, 1987, p. 81). Women seem more cautious about entering marriage and more willing to leave a marriage that is not working (Edwards & Demo, 1991).

Concurrent with these trends, women—excepting the cohort of baby boom mothers born in the 1930s—have decreased both the number of children they parent and the portion of their lives devoted to child rearing (Gee & Kimball, 1987). The latter decrease stems partly from the recent dramatic increase in the number of multiple births, mostly to older mothers (Canadian Press, 1993).

The net result of these changes is that, while the vast majority of women (and men) still get married, they have more options than did married people in earlier generations to protect their individual interests.

Becoming a Couple

When individuals are enduringly attracted to each other, they usually consider making the relationship permanent via marriage. In arriving at this decision, each of them assesses what will be gained and lost by doing

Median Age at Family Life-Course Events and Years Spent in Life Stages, Canadian Female Birth Cohorts

	Birth Cohort			
	1841–50	1901–10	1931–40	1951–60
Median age				
First Marriage	26.0	23.3	21.1	22.5
First Birth	28.0	25.0	22.9	24.5
Last Birth	40.0	29.1	29.1	26.3
Empty Nest[a]	60.1	49.1	49.1	46.3
Widowhood	59.5	61.3	67.2	69.9
Death of Women	64.3	67.3	79.4	82.2
Years spent				
Between marriage and first birth	2.0	1.7	1.8	2.0
Raising dependent children	32.1	24.1	26.2	21.8
Married, with no dependent children	−0.6	12.2	18.1	23.6
In widowhood	4.8	6.0	12.2	12.3

Source: E. M. Gee and M. M. Kimball (1987), *Women and Aging*, Orlando: Harcourt Brace Jovanovich , p. 83.
[a]Age of mother when last child is age 20.

so. The gains are easier to determine than the losses. This is partly because of individual factors: gains involve sharing personal interests and goals, the possibility of children, and the expectation that the couple can do some long-term planning. As well, societal norms and expectations stress the positive features of living together in heterosexual marriages. Never-married older adults report still receiving pressure from their match-making married friends long after they have made their preference for a single life quite clear (Norris, 1990).

The principal social psychological shift that occurs when people marry is a change in identity. Everything about themselves will be filtered through the new light of being part of a married couple. Both members leave behind the self-centered identity relied on and developed since childhood. They now must become other-directed, and think of themselves in relation to their spouse (Cox, 1990). Examples of couple identification are numerous. Some relatively simple transformations occur in occupational self-identity. When a man becomes a husband, for example, he is no longer "Janos the plumber" but "Janos the plumber who has some responsibility as a family wage earner." In his leisure life, as well, Janos's self-identity as an amateur actor places him as the actor attached to his wife, Mary.

Marital Adjustment

Adapting to the role of married person, or "marital adjustment," as it is called by family researchers, is dependent on a wide range of personal and social factors. Nett (1988, p. 233) defines marital adjustment as "the process of resolving conflict and achieving need fulfillment to the satisfaction of both partners." Conflict is inevitable in any close relationship—there will always be conflicting interests and a reluctance to sacrifice these. Nevertheless, some researchers have not explicitly acknowledged this. Rice (1990) discusses the importance of subsuming individual needs, at times, for the good of the couple, but does not address the process that leads to this end.

For at least one researcher (Nett, 1988), a couple can be considered well adjusted if most of the time the partners' interactions lead to mutual satisfaction. This does not mean they must get along most of the time. Some couples find arguing mutually satisfying. Couples can also adjust to situations that are not satisfying; thus, adjustment becomes the means, not the end, in a process in which satisfaction is the objective (Rice, 1990). In the discussion below, young partners manage a major conflict, and each emerges with a new appreciation for the position of the other. At the time, however, it is unlikely that either would have reported their conflict as "satisfying."

PAUL: Is it safe to discuss?

BETH: I think so, but you never know what's left over . . . We had one really bad fight. And then—I have to give you credit for this—you came to me and you said, "I know this is important to you and I don't understand why. But it's important to me that you get to do what really matters to you. So let's work out some way to do it." And once the pressure was off, you started to talk about your own concerns about looking after Willie, which I could understand, so I phoned my mom and asked her if she could come and stay here while I was away.   **(Cowan & Cowan, 1992, p. 189)**

Because satisfaction means different things to different people, it is best considered as something couples socially construct as they communicate with each other (Havemann & Lehtinen, 1990). This construction is facilitated by the attachment that gave rise to the decision to become a married couple. Close identity relationships, such as marriage, are sustained by a belief in global reciprocity, which supersedes the particular circumstances. This is true as long as, in balance, each member feels he or she is being treated fairly. A fair and reciprocal relationship, then, is one characterized by an interactive give-and-take that sometimes favors the interests of one individual, and sometimes those of the partner (Veevers, 1991; Havemann & Lehtinen, 1990).

The focus of this book is functioning couples dealing with their children as they grow into adults in their own right. These partners may, or may not, be in a first marriage, which may, or may not, be highly satisfying. As well, they communicate in a fashion that is reasonably functional for them, even if they may not necessarily consider themselves "well adjusted." Suffice it to say that couples must have achieved some mutual understanding on matters of sex, finances, and children for marital satisfaction to be potentially high. Nevertheless, couples who have only achieved partial agreement on these issues can still function reasonably well.

When there is less than full satisfaction among partners in one area, it can be increased on an individual level. For example, a father may derive great satisfaction from joining his children in sports not engaged in by their mother. Similarly, where need fulfillment is low in one area such as finances, enjoyment in another domain—like sex—can compensate.

When there is a poor working understanding on the main points and when strength in one area does not adequately compensate for weaknesses in others, spouses are in danger of becoming "married singles" (Cox, 1990). Having less and less in common, the partners increasingly revert to their former singles lifestyle. Sometimes couples carry on for many years in this fashion, and, of course, sometimes this leads to marital breakdown and divorce.

Marital adjustment is not static or unidirectional. One recent study, for example, showed that first-time married couples did not necessarily undergo a decline in marital satisfaction during the first year (Huston, McHale, & Crouter, 1986). Satisfaction was dependent on partners' assessments of the social and emotional dimensions of their interactions and only minimally on behavioral issues, such as who made dinner or did the laundry. It also appeared that first-year results could be predicted by signs of negative affect noticed in the first few months of marriage. This was true regardless of whether the couple had cohabited prior to marriage or had become parents within the first year. Thus, it seems that the quality of a marital couple's interactions is a more powerful predictor of satisfaction than are the circumstances surrounding their marriage.

In a similar vein, other researchers have found a difference between surface, or expressed, feelings and subsurface feelings, which do not get expressed and affect the couple's expectations for each other (Hochschild & Machung, 1989). The principal concern in this work was "the second shift": the extra time the woman in dual-income partnerships often put in at home dealing with household and parenting duties in excess of the effort contributed by her partner. The amount of extra work the woman did at home was great enough to constitute a second shift on top of her paid work. A clear sticking point for the couple was whether the man contributed in an equitable way (Hochschild & Machung, 1989). The man's behavior, however, was an outgrowth of what the couple's surface and subsurface feelings were regarding equity in housework and parenting. Marital adjustment was eased and satisfaction increased when surface and subsurface feelings matched within individuals and between partners. This matching, of course, may not appear spontaneously between members of a couple. It is likely to involve considerable negotiation, as husbands and wives clarify their positions and work toward an equitable distribution of tasks.

When a good emotional grounding can be established between them, partners are better situated to withstand the behavioral and circumstantial assaults that will follow through the years. Recall the family situation we described in Chapter 1 involving Margaret, Joe's sister. Just prior to the birth of her first child, she and her husband, Wayne, found themselves without functional living arrangements. So they asked Margaret's mother, Rachel, to let Margaret and the baby live with her until their house was ready.

In getting to this point in their relationship, Margaret and Wayne had to discuss and resolve a number of very important issues: whether they were sufficiently satisfied with their relationship that they wanted to get married; whether they wanted to have children; and whether, given their housing problems, the benefits of temporarily moving in with Rachel justified the potential strain on their relationship with her. The couple was able to weather the tensions that ultimately arose in this situation because they agreed on their shared objectives and the means for accomplishing them. As such, their adjustment was good, their marital satisfaction was relatively high, and asking for Rachel's help did not precipitate a lasting crisis. As couples move through their family life cycle, the behavior of either individual and the circumstances they face as couples have an impact on marital satisfaction (Lasswell & Lasswell, 1991).

The Social Context of Parenthood

Over the last 30 years, real family income in North America has dropped, and, increasingly, both spouses have contributed significantly to that income (Canadian Press, 1991; Nett, 1988). It is a bitter pill for couples to swallow that they are working harder and still doing less well than their parents did in similar occupations and on single incomes. It also puts them under more pressure. This drop in the standard of living has only recently been documented. Previously, young couples could only suspect it had occurred as they listened to their parents' stories about the financial support the parents had provided to multiple generations of their own families. The case of Joan's father, discussed in Chapter 1, and the help he gave to his parents and children, is not unusual for a man in his age cohort, i.e., born just after World War I.

Survey research by Pittman and Lloyd (1988, p. 53) examined the pressures on contemporary families by assessing the impact of stress, social support, and family resources on the quality of family life, where "quality" was subdivided into the domains of marital quality, parental satisfaction, and life satisfaction. They found that, while income was not a good predictor of level of life satisfaction, perceived financial stress was. Ironically, the number of children living at home was not perceived as a stressor in relation to life satisfaction; in fact, children appeared to buffer the effects of financial and relationship stressors.

Pittman and Lloyd (1988) found that marital satisfaction was higher when there were no children in the home. They also found marital satisfaction levels were higher for fathers than for mothers, but suspect this merely reflects differential involvement in the parenting role. They concluded that stress in one's home life and financial stress had the strongest negative effects on marital satisfaction. Either of these stressors is likely to be exacerbated by perceptions of inequity in support given and received within the couple relationship. Perceptions of support vary by family structure, generation the partner grew up in, culture and differences between individuals.

Another study (Fine, McKenry, Donnelly, & Voydanoff, 1992) looked for differences in perceived adjustment of parents and children by family structure, race, and gender. Using a subsample of a national study, the researchers questioned 397 respondents as to how satisfied they were with their lives. They reported that African-American males were less satisfied than white males, respondents from stepfather families were less satisfied than those from intact families, African-Americans from stepfather families were more likely to report being depressed than were whites from stepfather families, and females were more likely to be depressed than were males (Fine et al., p. 123).

In a study (McAdoo, 1988) involving intact eastern U.S. families, 40 of whom were African-American and 44 of whom were white, differences in parenting roles between fathers from each group were not apparent. African-American and white fathers, as well as their wives, were similarly involved in family decision making, and each racial group and sex generally were found to be nurturing of their children. McAdoo suggested that his research and other similar studies show that middle-class and well-to-do African-American fathers are very similar to their white counterparts.

In his study of 48 Irish fathers, their spouses, and infant children, Nugent (1991) found that those fathers who were young, rated their marital relationship highly, modified their work schedules, and participated in household tasks were more likely than other fathers to be actively involved in care of their infant child. Nugent (p. 483) also found evidence suggesting that fathers who actively participated in child care found this reflected positively in cognitive growth of their children at one year of age. Nugent concludes that, compared to earlier generations, Irish fathers are showing a pattern of increased parental involvement that is consistent with that in other Western cultures.

The above studies suggest that, when socioeconomic differences are accounted for, culture and race explain much less than we once believed about the parenting involvement of fathers. The increase in involvement is the good news; the bad news is that it is often a slow and painful process (Cowan & Bronstein, 1988). Indeed, some would suggest that the discrepancy between male and female roles in parenthood lends credence to "the hypothesis that each marriage is actually two marriages—his and hers"—because

> (1) new parents, when compared with themselves before childbirth and with non-parents . . . have more gender-specialized arrangements, with women involved more in childcare and men with employment; (2) spouses' primary self-perceptions begin to diverge after becoming parents, with women's sense of being "parent" increasing more than men's, which remains "partner"; and (3) the first two factors, plus any discrepancy in childrearing attitudes held by the couple (and only discovered at this time), increase conflict and *may* decrease marital satisfaction (Nett, 1988, p. 250).

Hochschild and Machung (1989) cite figures suggesting that, on average, a U.S. mother who works outside the home does one more month of housework per year than her husband and the father of their children. Within that "second shift," it is the mother who is responsible for keeping the family organized. It is Mom who typically gets everyone else out the door on time. The resentment caused by this inequity means diminished marital satisfaction among women (Hochschild & Machung, 1989).

The women's marital satisfaction was lessened because of the inequity in home responsibilities that exists specifically because women feel more responsible for home and children than men do. Further, when a father does help in this area, the "work" he takes on is more likely to be pleasurable (e.g., taking the kids tobogganing), leaving the more dreary chores (e.g., grocery shopping) to the mother. Even when a woman manages to negotiate shared labor with her husband, the outcome is likely to be less than satisfactory. As Hochschild and Machung (1989) quote one of the families in their study:

Evan and I eventually divided the labor so that I do the upstairs and Evan does the downstairs and the dog. So the dog is my husband's problem. But

when I was getting the dog outside and getting Joey ready for childcare, and cleaning up the mess of feeding the cat, and getting the lunches together, and having my son wipe his nose on my outfit so I would have to change—then I was pissed! I felt that I was doing *everything*. All Evan was doing was getting up, having coffee, reading the paper, and saying, "Well, I have to go now," and often forgetting the lunch I'd bothered to make.   (p. 44)

Becoming Parents

Apart from the decision to become a couple in the first place, perhaps the family life cycle transition requiring the most adjustment is the transition to parenthood. Palkovitz (1988, p. 3) has noted that

> if one applies the Holmes and Rahe (1967) Social Readjustment Scale to the transition to parenthood, the result is instructive. A conservative estimate is that a new parent would experience 339 life-change units. A more liberal application of the scale results in an estimated accumulation of 634 life-change units.

The situation couples face when deciding that they want to become parents is quite different from the one they are likely to encounter as they raise their children into young adulthood. Nevertheless, it is important to consider how these two family life cycle stages are linked, in our efforts to understand the development of intergenerational attachments. As we will see in Chapter 3, parents confront both freedom from everyday parenting when their grown children leave home, and the loss of that freedom if these children find it necessary to return to the nest. In order to make sense of the dilemma faced by these middle-age couples, we need to consider what was at stake for them as they tried to become parents.

Although the adjustment to parenthood is difficult, marital adjustment for the involuntarily childless carries with it complications that parents never have to face. Couples who want to become parents but cannot do so because of infertility experience a transition to nonparenthood. This can be extremely difficult in a society where there is a strong expectation that couples will raise children (Matthews & Martin Matthews, 1986; Sandelowski, Holditch-Davis, & Harris, 1990). Research suggests that it is even more difficult when perinatal loss or stillbirth has occurred. These couples may feel like parents even though they were not able to bring an infant home from the hospital. Well-meaning friends, relatives, and researchers, however, rarely acknowledge that a transition to parenthood has occurred (Ilse, 1982; Leroy, 1988).

Other couples become parents under unusual circumstances or at a time not expected by society (i.e., "off-time" parenting). For instance, they may wait until their mid-30s to have children, try for ten years or more before being able to conceive and give birth, adopt children, or become stepparents. New parents who have come through any of these processes experience a transition to parenthood that is not covered well in the literature. When researchers consider nonstandard parenting experiences (Sussman, 1988), the focus is usually on unwanted teen pregnancies.

In studying marital satisfaction, researchers take their sample from people in the most "typical" circumstances they can find. For instance, Belsky and Rovine (1990) sampled middle-class families composed of young couples married an average of four years who had biological children. This kind of research provides some control over intervening variables but, as the researchers themselves concede (see Belsky & Rovine, 1990), many parents are in different situations from those in their sample. One especially notable limitation of research like this is its focus on white, middle-class samples.

Studies of this kind are also limited by their focus on the couple in isolation from the broader social context. The partners themselves control only a portion of their own marital adjustment. They are very much influenced by external social factors. Fischer (1988), for example, draws our attention to the impact of kin on marital adjustment among new parents. The most influential are most often the new grandparents, particularly the maternal grandparents. As we will see in Chapter 4, a supportive relationship between the new parents and grandparents can make the transition to parenthood much easier. Conversely, if there is conflict between maternal and paternal grandparents, particularly grandmothers, the young couple may face even greater challenges in adjusting to parenthood.

It must be kept in mind, then, that the social context has an impact on marital adjustment during the transition to parenthood. The literature has tended to focus only on the couple relationship. Another limitation of the existing literature is its assumption that difficulties inherent in marital adjustment during the transition to parenthood inevitably lead to declines in marital satisfaction. In a state-of-the-art paper, Belsky and

Pensky (1988) challenged this conventional wisdom. In making their argument, these researchers drew upon the work of others who have asked if, in the absence of a control group, it is possible to determine whether the cause of declines in marital satisfaction was parenthood or simply couple maturation (White & Booth, 1985). Subsequent studies using control groups (Cowan et al., 1985) lend support to the conclusion that "couples with children differ from childless couples in the degree, and usually not the direction, of change" in marital satisfaction (Belsky & Pensky, p. 137).

Studies like this provide us with a description of differences in marital satisfaction between parents and nonparents, but the explanation for these differences remains unclear. Couples may differ on many variables other than parenthood, such as age, ethnicity, income, and relationship history, that may have an impact on marital quality. In addition, the motivation of couples to bear children or to remain childless is rarely considered. Did those couples who became parents plan to do so? Is the control group composed of voluntarily childless couples as well as those trying to conceive and those who have had long-term experience with infertility? As Belsky and Pensky (1988) point out, such within-group differences may make almost meaningless any comparison between childless couples and those who have made the transition to parenthood.

Belsky and Pensky's own data do support the view that declines in marital satisfaction typically, but not inevitably, occur and suggest factors that are most likely to lead to such declines. These factors include parenthood—but also the passage of marital time and role (motherhood versus fatherhood). Other researchers have confirmed the finding that low marital satisfaction is not improved by becoming parents and noted that it is worsened when the couple feels stress about their perceived competence as parents (Wallace & Gotlib, 1990).

A recent study further addressed the question of whether marital satisfaction declines or improves with the transition to parenthood (Belsky & Rovine, 1990). Couples were interviewed when the wife was in the last trimester of pregnancy and again when the child was 3, 9, and 36 months of age. Because the results failed to provide clear answers, the researchers concluded that questioning the impact of parenthood on marital satisfaction was inappropriate. They maintained that it would be more fruitful to ask about the origins of individual differences in marital change during this period.

Analyses showed that prenatal data were predictive only when "demographic, personality, and marital variables were simultaneously considered, but not when they were separately employed to distinguish between marriages that deteriorated and improved in quality" (Belsky & Rovine, 1990, p. 16). This suggests that the nature of change is driven by a multiplicity of factors. The analyses of postnatal data were more predictive in the case of wives than husbands. It appeared that the impact of child temperament through the first year was felt most strongly by the mother. Generally, the more disruptive the baby's eating and sleeping patterns, the more likely it was that the mother would experience declines in love and increased conflict with her husband during this time.

Other recent work (Mebert, 1991) lends further insight into the prediction of how well couples will manage during the transition to parenthood. Mebert notes that the transition to parenting typically begins not with the birth of the baby but with the decision to have one. In the case of unplanned pregnancies, however, the transition starts much closer to the birth of the baby or not until that point (Mebert, 1991, p. 47). In cases of adoption, the transition may begin when the couple attempts, unsuccessfully, to have a biological child, and continues through the time they spend seeking to adopt. But as we saw in the story that opened this chapter, when the adoption actually occurs, it can dramatically compress the amount of time available for couples to adjust to their new role.

Mebert's (1991) findings suggest that a couple's response to becoming parents depends, in part, on when they decided that they wanted to have a baby. Couples in this study who planned their pregnancies, and did not encounter undue difficulty in having the baby, had a year or so to adjust to the anticipated change in family status. By the time the baby arrived, these parents could make use of what, by then, were existing adjustment strategies. Mebert considers these couples to have been in an assimilation mode.

Couples who were surprised to discover that the wife was pregnant or endured years of trying to conceive followed by years of going through the trials of the adoption process, were much less likely to be in assimilation mode. Other research supports the view that couples with unwanted or unplanned pregnancies may well experience a lengthy struggle to adjust and some difficulty in discarding their previous identity as child-free or "once infertile always infertile" (Sandelowski, Holditch-Davis, & Harris, 1992). For different reasons, adoptive parents may have equal difficulty altering their former self-perceptions (Daly, 1992). Their experience has been long, impossible to plan, and fraught with disappointment, followed by the excitement of the adoption. Adoptive parents often have traveled such a winding, up-and-down path on the way to parenthood that while they may have a reservoir of proven adjustment strategies, these may not apply well to parenthood.

In short, couples who are stunned to find they are parents and those who have trouble believing it has finally happened may each find themselves in what Mebert (1991) has labeled the accommodation mode. Such parents struggle to work out adjustment strategies as they go. Their success is likely to be determined by negotiation and open communication. The potential for trouble down the road when such communication is constrained is evident in the comments of this adoptive couple:

HUSBAND: Everyone believes that "it [infertility] won't happen to us," and until it does, I don't think that they will ever understand. When I realized that the only way we were going to have our own children was through adoption—even to the day that we picked up our little girl, I was really very tentative. I really wanted to—but I think I went along with it because it meant a lot to her.

WIFE: That's a terrible thing to say! [nervously laughs]

HUSBAND: Well, . . . I was in agreement, but I was in all honesty very tentative about the whole thing. [uncomfortable silence]   (Daly, 1992, p. 113)

In general, Mebert suggests that getting through the transition to parenthood is easier for couples who have a reservoir of adjustment strategies they can assimilate into their lives as parents and who can, when necessary, become accommodative in adapting to unforeseen circumstances. A good example might be assimilative parents who very suddenly find themselves scrambling to accommodate to the first serious illness experienced by their child.

In sum, the process of marital adjustment during the transition to parenthood includes a myriad of influences. The motivation to become parents, and the ability to realize that objective, are the first steps in a much more complex exchange. The other characteristics of the couple, and their relationship with each other, will largely predict the effect of arriving children on their marital satisfaction. Kin, particularly the children's grandparents, tend to be supportive influences; the relation-

Reprinted with special permission of King Features Syndicate.

ship they had with the new parents before this new stage will determine if this happens. When children arrive, they are new players in a game that is already well underway.

When we speak in Chapter 3 of the potential for improved marital satisfaction when children are launched, the explicit assumption is that rearing young children is not conducive to high levels of nuptial bliss. Part of the ongoing conversation couples engage in as they raise and launch children depends on the balance of marital power: how it was initially established and how time and circumstances have caused it to vary.

Support from Grandparents

The interactions between spouses while they manage as a couple and adjust as parents do not occur in a vacuum. Parents can, and do, receive support from outside their nuclear structure. Friends and the children's grandparents, for example, are essential supplements to spousal support in times when circumstances are strained. Grandparents are an obvious source of regular or back-up child care. Grandparents are also able to act as baby-sitters when the young-adult "boomerang" children come home again. In times of crisis, a therapeutic role is often taken on by those who become "significant grandparents" (Veevers, 1991, p. 343). In a newspaper article on boomerang children, a widowed grandmother said that when her daughter, a divorced single parent laid off from her job, returned home and then was joined by her son when he lost his job, she had no idea how she would manage. Now, although she feels her new housemates do not do enough housework, and her son's late night lifestyle bothers her, overall there is reciprocity and a relationship she values. She says having her children back in the house keeps her young and provides her with companionship and help with the housework. (Scott, 1992, p. D1).

People like this widow have accepted, at least temporarily, becoming a therapeutic parent again. In return, they can enjoy companionship not experienced since becoming widowed.

Support from Friends

Friends are particularly useful when the source of strain is something external to the family that, in its consequences, has an impact on the family. Young partners, seeking a balance in their maturing relationship, often find that friends compensate for support not provided by their spouse, and supplement the support they do receive from their spouse. Couples often find support in friends who also have children. Women, especially, are likely to develop a close relationship with female friends who are also mothers. Friends can provide confirmation and reassurance from peers at a time when the partners are feeling their way as parents, and with each other.

While it is not their principal function, the role friends can play when there is a crisis is also important. When a marriage begins to unravel, for example, they can provide invaluable support to a newly single parent struggling to sort out which relations should be maintained and which jettisoned.

Just as critically, friends can provide support when family members are not available, as a recent experience of the authors illustrates. Joan Norris's spouse underwent overnight surgery in an out-of-town hospital. Their children's paternal grandfather and his new wife spend the winter in Florida and so were not in the country. The maternal grandfather did not want to venture too far from his wife, who is confined to a nursing home. So Joe Tindale's wife, Helen, spent the night at the Norris home caring for Joan's three children while Joe stayed home with the Tindale kids. In the morning, Joe took over when Helen had to leave for work before the children were off to school. Joe got all five kids out the door and dropped off at their respective school bus stops and nursery school activities before continuing on to work himself.

Couples also need support from loved ones, including friends, when they experience a work crisis. This was reflected in research by Tindale (1989) with a sample of unemployed factory workers. He conducted interviews with 120 laid-off male tire plant employees, ranging in age from the late teens to 64. Each respondent was a father and involved in an ongoing relationship with his spouse. Relative to some other unemployed persons, they had high incomes; this was because they qualified for more than 90% of their income in unemployment insurance benefits during the year following the layoff.

When asked how losing their jobs had affected relations with their spouse, respondents were likely to say they argued more now than before the layoff, at the same time as their partner had become an even more important source of support. One man put it this way:

I need her sympathy more now, but we fight more.
(55-year-old man with two children)

Others replied similarly to the man who said,

[W]e care about each other, we need each other more often than before the layoff for support.   (27-year-old man with one child)

Friends are an especially important source of support when the stress affecting a friend includes all of their family as well. As one worker said,

I am relying more on my friends and family for keeping my spirits up.
(58-year-old man with one child)

Unfortunately, when a person is experiencing unemployment, poor morale and strapped finances may impede access to the support relationship:

I am losing a lot of friends because I am not in the mood for socializing. People don't like people who are unemployed and have no money.
(58-year-old man with three children)

I miss my friends from work a lot. These were people I knew for most of my [more than 20 years] work history . . . We had a lot of things in common, and we had a good working relationship. We don't have the opportunity to get together such as work afforded us. I keep in touch with a couple of them but not the whole group.   (59-year-old man with six children)

These examples illustrate that friends, who often are associated with one's employment, play a vital role in supplementing spousal support when work circumstances change for the worse.

Family Life Cycle Influences on Marital Satisfaction

Since, as Schumm and Bugaighis (1986) point out, it is not news that family life cycle has an influence on marital quality, they examined the marital career to determine some of the particulars of the family life cycle effect. They report that across all stages, family life cycle accounted for only 8% of variance in marital satisfaction. Among the subsample of working mothers with preschool children, however, family life cycle stage accounted, both directly and indirectly, for 25% of the variance in marital satisfaction (Schumm & Bugaighis, p. 167).

We can also reasonably expect that the nature of this life cycle effect would vary by generation. The relationship between family time and work time is a case in point. Prior to World War II very few women worked outside the home, especially when they had preschool children. Thus, women were able to devote a great deal of time to child rearing and housekeeping. The result was that parents felt entitled to address their own needs first without feeling the needs of their children were being neglected.

In the last 20 years, with more than 60% of adult women working for pay, parents have focused their child-rearing efforts on "quality time." Apart from weekends, the bulk of this "quality time" is spent getting children up and off to day care or school in the morning, picking them up for supper, and putting them to bed. In the morning, it is a struggle for everyone to wake up and get moving. At supper, everyone is tired and hungry. Too often quality time becomes the "arsenic hour." This has created family situations in which "child monsters" rule.

A flexible balance is required if parents and children are going to be able to understand each other's needs and address them over the span of their relationship (Lasswell & Lasswell, 1991). As children grow into adolescence, the nature of parental authority needs to become less hierarchical and more "permeable," or flexible (Edwards & Demo, 1991, p. 172). This strategy allows adolescents to have the opportunity to try on independence and be able to make mistakes within the safety of parental supervision.

Adolescent Children and Marital Satisfaction

We have already noted that becoming a parent is associated with a decline in marital satisfaction, but the specific predictors of this decline are still unclear. We do not know, for example, whether number of children makes a difference. And while some studies suggest preschool children can have a particularly detrimental impact on marital satisfaction, particularly on the mother's during the first year, others indicate that adolescents could have an even worse effect (Gecas & Seff, 1990).

Perhaps the one point that is clear at this stage in the research literature is that there is a need for more studies on the reciprocal relationship between parents, their adolescent children, and the impact of this relationship on marital satisfaction (Gecas & Seff, 1990). Research has underscored this point with particular reference to the effect of parent–child interaction on the self-esteem of each affected generation (Demo, Small, & Savin-Williams, 1987). When parents and adolescents report a good parent–child relationship, characterized by good communication and high levels of interaction, high levels of self-esteem are also noted. However, the views of parents and children on whether the relationship is good do not always coincide (Demo, Small, & Savin-Williams, 1987).

Other research suggests that changes in a marriage may simply be coincident with children's adolescent years (Steinberg & Silverberg, 1987). The finding that "women's, but not men's, midlife concerns are predictive of marital satisfaction" (Steinberg & Silverberg, p. 713) is consistent with the observation that women in mid-life are more likely than men to question their marital identity and find it wanting. With their children grown up and requiring less attention, women have more time and energy for considering such issues and may also have greater attachment to occupational careers.

The life cycle perspective shows promise in helping researchers find out whether the age of the children makes a difference in the marital satisfaction of parents (Gecas & Seff, 1990). Without good longitudinal data, however, the issue cannot be resolved, and, to date, very little such data exist.

Summary and Conclusion

This chapter has focused on the process whereby two individuals become a couple and considered the factors that affect the quality of the couple's relationship when they become parents. There is uncertainty in the research regarding which variables are most predictive of marital satisfaction. This is less important, however, than the certainties in the literature: Partners' marital satisfaction is affected by their becoming parents and by their experiencing difficulty in becoming parents; there are gender and life cycle effects on marital satisfaction; family relationships are mediated by economic variables such as labor force participation and income.

Each dimension of the transition to parenthood provides numerous opportunities for, and just as many potential obstacles to, reciprocal exchange relations. As families reconstruct themselves after divorce, as parents adjust to children, it is the attachment characteristic of their relationships that enables them to consider their reciprocal exchange relations in a global or life cycle perspective.

With marriage comes identity change, and this is the beginning of marital adjustment—multidimensional, ongoing, mutual need fulfillment—in which satisfaction is socially constructed. A decline in marital satisfaction over a period following marriage and a further decline following parenthood are typical, although neither is inevitable. The impact of becoming a parent often is felt more acutely by mothers; fathers are thought to be less affected because, typically, they are less involved than mothers in the parenting role.

What affects the marital satisfaction of parents? Beyond the likelihood that simply being a parent has a dampening effect, marital satisfaction can be affected by virtually any phenomena that impinge on the day-to-day wellbeing of parents. Our interpretation of the research suggests that financial stress and stress at home are two important factors that will precipitate declines in marital satisfaction. Family structure and ethnicity/culture also play a role.

Perceived support during these difficult years in the family life cycle does make a difference and can, depending on the circumstances, sustain satisfaction levels for the parents. Support can come from a variety of sources. Grandparents and friends are some of the most common sources of support. Children, although often a principal source of declines in parental marital satisfaction, can also serve as valuable sources of support. The first source of support for a parent is a spouse. It should be remembered, though, that no one, not even a spouse, can be everything for someone else. Not surprisingly, then, even parents with very supportive spouses normally can be expected to seek additional or different support from others in their network.

When a couple is experiencing financial and relationship stress, children can act as a buffer. They can be someone to talk to, someone to invest yourself in, or simply a distraction. Parents often spend so much of their nonwork time caring for children and paying the bills that the marital relationship, while needing attention, receives only the bare essentials. This is clearly the situation in which Stephanie and Art now find themselves:

STEPHANIE: **We're managing Linda really well. But with Art's promotion from teacher to principal, and my going back to work and feeling guilty about being away from Linda, we don't get much time for** *us.* **I try to make time for the two of us at home but there's no point in making time to be with somebody if he doesn't want to be with you. Sometimes when we finally get everything done and Linda is asleep, I want to sit down and talk, but Art says this is a perfect opportunity to get some preparation done for one of his teachers' meetings. Or he starts to fix one of Linda's toys—things that apparently are more important to him than spending time with me.**

ART: **That does happen. But Stephanie's wrong when she says that those things are more important to me than she is. The end of the day is just not my best time to start a deep conversation. I keep asking her to get a sitter so that we can go out for a quiet dinner, but she always finds a reason not to. It's like being turned down for a date week after week.**

(Cowan & Cowan, 1992, p. 82)

In providing support ranging from child care and car loans to providing a roof for "boomerang" children, grandparents extend help that very few others could or would. Grandparents do this because it is part of their global reciprocity and attachment to their children and grandchildren. They, too, then, are stake holders in the marital adjustment of their children.

Friends can either compensate for a lack of spousal and grandparent support, or they can function as supplementary support. They can step in during crises such as marriage breakdown or unemployment. More commonly, they extend support on a day-to-day basis, helping out with the never-ending litany of little things that can overwhelm parents.

The marital adjustment partners experience through the years of becoming parents and raising children to adulthood is one phase in their family life cycle. Through this period several new relationships develop, such as those between parent and child, and between grandparent and grandchild. Peer relationships for couples are also transformed by the parenting experience. In each case, long-term attachment allows people to work toward lifelong reciprocity. In the next chapter, we begin to see how reciprocal relationships change again as children become semi-autonomous adults and parents begin to think about spending more time as a couple.

Parenting Adult Children: Unlikely to Be Home Alone

Marcus and Theresa had worked hard for 30 years in the city. The day had come for Marcus to retire. Theresa had worked in the home and by now their two children had moved out and started families of their own. They decided their retirement savings would go further if they moved to a small town where the cost of living was more reasonable than it was in the city. They sold their home and bought a two-bedroom house. There was some money to spare provided by the cost differential between city and town. These savings paid off their consumer debt. Marcus and Theresa were ready to move on to the next phase of their lives, being by themselves again for the first time in over 20 years.

Six years after moving, Theresa became ill with cancer; after two years of various treatments, she died. For the next year or so Marcus was on his own and alone in the house. It was not what he had anticipated, but he managed.

All of this changed when his daughter, Lisa, returned to the nest, newly separated, two children in tow. She had little in the way of savings and needed to move back in with her father while she reorganized her life and accumulated some savings.

Marcus was upset that his daughter was in these straits. He wanted to help, but this had not been part of his thinking when he and Theresa bought a two-bedroom house. He did not have two or three extra bedrooms.

The solution was amicable, but not reached without some negotiation. Marcus spent a considerable amount of money to have the basement finished and a *bathroom installed. His arrangement with Lisa was that she could stay two years, but then Marcus expected her to be in her own home again. He did not want to have children running around his house for the rest of his retirement.*

Shortly after Lisa and the children moved into the renovated basement, Marcus met and became attracted to Rachel. She had been widowed for 10 years and met Marcus through a mutual friend. Within six months Marcus and Rachel had decided they wanted to get married. However, they both had cared for a sick spouse for a couple of years and both had a house that was their principal estate to pass on to their respective children. Astounding themselves in the process, they spent an additional couple of months working out a marriage arrangement that maintained their separate estates for their respective children. Rachel said that if she could get the contract finally settled, marriage itself would be easy.

At the time they got married, Lisa had been living with her father for about a year. During his adult life Marcus had lived with Theresa, Theresa and their children, just Theresa, without Theresa, with Lisa and the two grandchildren, and now with Rachel, Lisa, and the two grandchildren. Rachel had not had any boomerang children, but she had been widowed, and now she was getting used to living with a new husband, a stepdaughter, and two step-grandchildren. Clearly this was a time for tact, good communication, and flexibility with regard to personal turf!

It did take a few months for everyone to become comfortable with each other, but gradually Marcus, Rachel, Lisa, and her children settled into a familiar routine. About a year after Marcus and Rachel were married, Lisa and her kids moved to a rented house. Less than a year later, Marcus had a stroke and died several days later. His children, particularly Lisa, have remained close to Rachel. Rachel's four children and her stepchildren get together several times a year. When everyone is there, the dinner table has to seat Rachel, six children, five children-in-law, and ten grandchildren.

This family situation is based on the experience of some members of Joseph's family. It reveals family life cycle transitions often experienced by middle-aged and older couples. All parents experience some version of the empty nest. The nature of the emptying and the possibilities for refill, however, have expanded over the last generation. Retirement at younger ages has become more widespread, and people are living longer (Novak, 1993). Divorce rates have climbed for both younger and older couples (Novak, 1993). The possibilities for renegotiating family relationships have correspondingly expanded.

In the last chapter, we saw that young couples embark on a series of important undertakings. After making a commitment to each other, they must make other major decisions. Will they become parents? What kind of home can they make their own? Each decision requires negotiation and affects relationships with others, particularly with extended family and friends.

Ongoing relationships include a social exchange process (Treas & Bengtson, 1987). Asking friends to help drywall the basement because the guest bedroom just became a nursery carries on the give-and-take already shared with these people, but with a difference. The debt undertaken in this case is for a third party: a child. Asking parents for a loan to buy a car because one partner is now home with a baby while the other partner continues to commute on public transit is also likely, where feasible, to meet with a favorable response. Nevertheless, the request challenges a North American norm (Ward, Logan, & Spitze, 1992) that parents will not, except in extraordinary circumstances, continue to support their adult children. It also delays the transition to independence that adult children struggle to achieve. Relationships and circumstances do change when children move out to begin their own adult lives, but this does not mean they have become fully independent.

Negotiating New Roles

Before young couples become parents, they are often concerned with finding secure employment or establishing careers. They are often short on time and money. Later, when children arrive, resources are further stretched. Parents may see no improvement in their financial status and time available to each other for many years, perhaps until the children complete their education and leave the parental home. Suddenly, there is time and money to spare, and decisions must be made about the use of these resources (Matras, 1990).

The newfound time can be used in a number of ways. Mothers who have stayed at home with children may decide to reenter the work force; this decision will hinge upon opportunities for employment as well as the adequacy of an individual woman's education and skills (Calzavara, 1988). The growing number of working mothers who have struggled to manage the "second shift" (Hochschild & Machung, 1989) will feel relief when they need cope only with a single shift. Even though fathers are less likely than their wives to have been homemakers when their children were young, we saw in the last chapter that fathers are increasingly involved in parenting. For those who invested considerable time and effort in child rearing, the newly found time can be applied to career advancement or making the most of life outside of work.

At this point college educations have been paid for, the children have finally been launched, the mortgage may have been paid off, and other consumer debts minimized. So there is likely to be more discretionary income available to parents, raising new questions: Can they begin to save for retirement or add to savings? Can they take a long vacation?

Underlying these specific decisions about time and money is a more general concern that couples must address: They must come to terms with a new stage in the family life cycle. Issues concerning individual needs and the needs of the couple relationship are likely to surface. Does either partner feel a need to devote more time to work? Do they have a sense that the relationship is changing? It is likely that many aspects of the couple's life together are in need of overhaul. Where do they go from here and how do they get there?

As a couple negotiates answers to these questions, they are likely to become aware of power differences between them. Thus, there may be considerable jockeying for position (Scanzoni, 1979). Resolving any differences is even more difficult in a society undergoing changes in gender relationships. When the marriage was young, traditional sex roles—father was the breadwinner; mother provided child care—may have been appropriate. Increased resources and a social climate that facilitates egalitarianism within the family threatens these roles, resulting in changes being negotiated by the couple. This can be seen in the comments of a 64-year-old retired real estate broker, Mr. Bernstein, who was interviewed as part of a study on the meaning of grandparenting (Norris & Tari, 1985). Mr. Bernstein and his wife had been married for 28 years at the time of the interview and had three grown children and a 10-year-old grandson:

[Life's] great. I am sort of retired but I have some investments in a little property and I putter around and we have enough money to live reasonably. My wife works three days a week and it pays for our holidays and special things and I think it keeps her interested. She talks of quitting and it would be lovely to not have her work interfering in our going away at times. But on the other hand I think her working the three days a week, she can enjoy the other four more.

It is clear, then, that family history and social history are important in understanding how couples cope with marriage in later life. Life-span theorists (e.g., Baltes, 1979) concur with this, and add that an individual's development interacts with these variables to necessitate changes in family strategies (Hagestad, 1981; Hareven, 1987). Decision making within each role transition takes the past into account. By the time a couple have seen their children through the front door, at least temporarily, they have many well-established strategies for dealing with change.

The Satisfying Marriage

Coping successfully with change is a major determinant of long-term satisfaction in marriage. Couples who remain together can expect some difficult times before they reach old age, mostly because of their children! Early in the marital relationship, happiness is at its peak, with spouses sharing many activities. Later, when children arrive, less time can be spent on the marriage; the result is declining marital satisfaction. By mid-life, happiness with the marriage declines again, especially for wives. Women can feel trapped by the dependency of their teenage children, the needs of increasingly frail parents, and the "clinginess" of their mates (Lowenthal, Thurner, & Chiriboga, 1975).

Early research on marital satisfaction suggested that this bleak picture only became bleaker for most couples (e.g., Pineo, 1968). Retirement for men and the launching of children for women were thought to produce even greater unhappiness, unalleviated by the possibility that the partners could now spend more time together. Researchers proposed that couples could only grow apart with age (Pineo, 1968).

Couples certainly can experience an "emotional divorce" by the time the children have grown up; they may remain together physically, but feel psychologically distant (Fitzpatrick, 1984). Recent evidence, however, suggests that this is not a typical pattern. It is more likely that couples will rebound and reorganize their relationship at the point when children are being launched from the family home. This process often results in increased marital happiness and can be seen as an upturn in satisfaction (Connidis, 1987; Lupri & Frideres, 1981). This has been the experience of Mr. Weber, a 65-year-old merchant still working full-time in his store. At the time that Mr. Weber was interviewed in the Norris and Tari (1985) grandparenting study, he and his wife had been married for 36 years and had two children and one grandchild:

When you are young you are out hustling to make a living and the wife has got problems and the husband has got problems, you are paying a mortgage on the house, paying this and clothing and shoes for the children.

[When you are older], you're financially more secure, you have less on your mind, your children are gone from your house and I think you are more or less at ease I would say as far as I'm concerned.

It is not surprising, then, that researchers have found satisfaction scores to be high in long-term marriages (Matras, 1990). This pattern appears related to the number of years a couple has invested in the relationship (Cassidy, 1985). One study found that 80% of couples married at least 50 years considered their relationship to have been happy from their wedding day to the present (Sporakowski & Axelson, 1984). Why is this the case? One explanation comes from a cognitive consistency perspective (Cassidy, 1985). People strive to be consistent in their thoughts and their actions. Couples married for a long time will seek an interpretation of their marital satisfaction that is consistent with the number of years they have invested in the relationship. Since they have stuck it out this long, they must have been happy!

A second reason for the happiness of long-term marriages is even simpler: Unhappy couples are likely to divorce before their children have left home. The result of this "selective survival" process may be a population of couples not characteristic of older people in general (Cassidy, 1985). Weihaus and Field (1988), for example, in a study of long-term marriages found none that had progressively deteriorated. Such a finding is unlikely at other points in the family life cycle. Most long-term couples showed a curvilinear or stable positive pattern in satisfaction. Individuals in these relationships communicated understanding, affection, and love, and were unlikely to criticize their partners or their marriages.

As these successfully married older adults can attest, good communication is vital in adapting to changing circumstances. In fact, the way in which members of a couple communicate about changing aspirations and perceptions of reality in their relationship can be characterized as an ongoing "conversation" (Rhyne, 1981). This conversation continues across the life span, facilitating any changes necessary for the smooth functioning of the relationship. Marital satisfaction can then be seen as a social construction, brought about by an ongoing process of communication.

In the Schleisners' relationship, for example (Norris, 1981), it is clear that each member of the couple has had different needs at different points in the marriage. Early on, Mr. Schleisner's career and interest in maintaining ties with his army friends required active social involvement from his wife. Late in the marriage, Mrs. Schleisner's poor health meant that her husband engaged in the quieter pursuits that she enjoyed. Mr. Schleisner feels that things have worked out well:

[We've] had a happy time in life. Fifty years in December we've been married. It's pretty good!

The first time I took her out, she was 15 and during that period—I went to university when I was 17—spent four years at the University of Toronto. Every social function that came up, I brought her over from St. Catharine's for it. No break in it at all!

I kept in touch with my Army buddies after I came back from Overseas. I got my wife interested in the Mess and the social functions. She convened parties for them at the Yacht Club and at the Army and so on.

[Since she's been sick], she does beautiful needlework, and loves that sort of thing. So now I turn my hand to a bit of wood carving and things that keep me busy. Last year I started soap stone.   (Norris, 1981)

When poor communication does occur in a long-term marriage, it may have been brought about by shifts in sex-linked traits (Zube, 1982). As couples reach middle age, there is evidence that men become less aggressive and more interested in personal satisfaction while women often become more aggressive and assertive about their perceived need for self-expression (Zube, 1982). It is not entirely clear whether these changes are intrinsic and developmental (e.g., Gutmann, 1978) or more a product of life events such as retirement. Whatever their cause, however, such changes are likely to have a profound effect on the marital "conversation." It will take some adjustment, for example, to understand the emerging expressiveness of a husband or the assertiveness of a wife.

If basic styles of communication change over the life of a marriage, there is great potential for misunderstanding. It is not surprising, then, that couples sometimes disagree on issues fundamental to their happiness. One such issue is the amount of emotional and tangible support spouses provide for one another. It is more likely in later life for couples to have differing views about this support (Depner & Ingersoll-Dayton, 1985). Old strategies regarding support that evolved out of the couple's communication in the first years of marriage are no longer relevant given new circumstances and personal needs. Thus, it becomes necessary to renegotiate, but if both are feeling relatively deprived and misunderstood, good communication becomes even more difficult.

The Effects of the Empty Nest

Probably the biggest change in role parents face at this point in the family life cycle is the departure of their children from the home. The research literature has traditionally defined this as the mother's problem and labeled it "empty nest syndrome." Although there is literature on the increasing involvement in parenting of fathers of young children, the literature on fathers has ignored the empty nest, considering it of no consequence for them.

A study indicating the limited durability of fathers in the role of primary caregiver is indicative of the family life cycle focus in this literature and the newness of the stay-at-home dad phenomenon (Radin, 1988). Others have explored difficulties encountered by stepfathers in becoming comfortable in the role: "It takes time" (Santrock, Sitterle, & Warshak, 1988). At the same time, the workplace is gradually acknowledging the phenomenon of fathers who are active, if not primary, caregivers, in the gradual spread of workplace benefits that give parents of either sex greater flexibility as they try to balance work and family responsibilities (Tindale, 1991; Catalyst, 1988).

In recent years the literature on empty-nest mothers has argued against the old shibboleth that this life transition automatically means the loss of a principal role and causes depression in women (Rovner, 1990). Indeed, a study of 1,890 married white persons aged 18 to 64 (Radloff, 1980) reported that empty-nest parents were actually *less* depressed than parents still residing with their children.

The point made above that women in middle age often become more assertive was echoed in a study that compared 25 empty-nest women to 25 women who were not yet at this point (Cooper & Gutmann, 1987).

The researchers found that the departure of children marked a significant psychological change, one "wherein post–empty nest women are more free to express some of the masculine qualities of assertion, aggression, and executive capacity which they had to repress in the service of parenthood" (p. 352).

While the research examples are limited, further studies suggest that ethnicity does not create significant variations in women's responses to the empty nest. Rogers and Markides (1989) reported findings on a sub-sample of 243 middle-aged (32–68 years) Mexican-American women. They found that these women had levels of well-being equal to those of other ethnic groups examined in the literature. In this sample, also, employed mothers were, on average, five years younger and less likely to express depressive or physical symptomatology than were nonemployed postparental mothers (p. 512).

The beneficial characteristics of employment for women is also reflected in a study of 238 middle-aged Caucasian women with varying employment and marital statuses (Barnett & Baruch, 1985). The results indicated that it is the character of role expectations and not the number of roles a person balances that is predictive of stress. Additionally, family role expectations were found to be more stressful than work role demands for these women. In fact, the study reported that "role conflict and role overload are strongly related to anxiety only among non-employed women" (p. 144).

Children moving out of the parental home does appear to be conducive to well-being in women and is suggestive of improved marital satisfaction for the couple. There is also research noting that this well-being is optimized when children physically move out but remain in close contact (White & Edwards, 1990). A reorganization such as this does not imply an end to parenting, but it does enable the middle-aged couple to consider new uses of their time and energy.

Overall then, the literature supports the idea of the empty nest as a source of freedom for many women, but it has not considered adequately the father's response to this life cycle stage. If a couple's approach to parenting has been similarly one-sided, the more assertive empty-nest woman will have to consider this in exploring how to move on in her marriage and her life. Having said this, while some older married couples may not agree about how much they support each other (Depner & Ingersoll-Dayton, 1985), others may be quite satisfied with their long-term marriages (Cassidy, 1985; Sporakowski & Hughston, 1978). The explanation for this probably lies in individuals' interpretations of events. When the children leave home, the balance of support given and received is disturbed at the same time as role transitions occur. To cope with this upheaval, people will minimize discordant perceptions of themselves and their long-term relationships. Those who are successful in this may show no differences in *level* of marital satisfaction even though they have largely reconstructed the *basis* on which that level of satisfaction depends.

Happy older couples may be thinking that, while much of what they have taken for granted in their lives is changing, it is changing for the better. They are able, for the first time in about 20 years, to direct more time to themselves and each other. The children set the trap, and the parents take the bait.

Are the Children Really Gone?

MR. ANDERSON: You see I wouldn't want my grandchildren to come into the house and live here, I wouldn't want that at all.

MRS. ANDERSON: That isn't a good thing anyway because it's too much, there's too much of an age gap and as you get older you just can't take the noise and the demanding and all that sort of thing anymore, you just can't.

MR. ANDERSON: We've got a good relationship. If we saw too much of our own kids it might be bad. See I would like for the kids to live on the same street so they could come without bringing their mother and dad. That's my idea. They could come in. I don't want to see my boy everyday. He's all right and he's doing fine but if the grandkids would come running in that would be lovely.
                                                    (Norris & Tari, 1985)

The Andersons, like most older couples, believe in "intimacy at a distance" (Connidis, 1989b; Wister, 1985): They would like regular contact with their children and grandchildren, but they do not want to live with them or to see them constantly. This is consistent with the idea that economic necessity, not reverence for the extended family, kept multiple generations under one roof in the past. In recent times of relative economic opportunity, independent households for young adult children and elderly kin have been promoted (Laslett, 1971). When households of multiple generations of adults do exist now, it can be argued that, just as in the last century, the arrangement stems from economic necessity (Stock, 1974; Glick & Lin, 1986). When the economic climate is favorable, the trend has been for earlier departures of children from the parental home (Matras, 1990). Independent living by both generations, then, is normative. Co-residency occurs and often works out well, but is not normative (Ward, Logan, & Spitze, 1992).

When children leave, it does not mean parents have parted with the role; it has simply become less immediate and, presumably, less demanding (Matras, 1990). Often the children are away temporarily at college or in the armed forces. They are simultaneously gone and not gone. Thus, the parents have been said to reside in "semiautonomous households" (Goldscheider & DaVanzo, 1986).

Children are physically out of the house, but they are not gone in terms of continued two-way giving of emotional support. (The direction of material support is normally parent-to-child until parents are well into their 70s and the children are in their 40s [Spitze & Logan, 1992].) Some research suggests that these ongoing relations may not be accompanied by much emotional satisfaction. A study that pooled three samples of community-dwelling older adults found that, while parents and children continued to provide mutual support after the children left home, they did not enjoy each other's company and the parental role was a vestigial part of the older person's social identity (Eisenhandler, 1992).

A study that investigated the need and feasibility of community programs for older parents found that they desire continued emotional support from their children but have to learn how to communicate and negotiate their dual needs of closeness and separateness (Blieszner & Mancini, 1987). Research that examined parent–child relations after a parent moves into close proximity with an adult child found that autonomy and dependency were important issues. The child's attachment feelings toward the parent eased the negotiating of a new phase in relations (Moss & Moss, 1992). The need for these negotiations, and the suggestion that some parents have difficulty negotiating the move away from hierarchical relationships toward those which are more egalitarian, are reflected in newspaper reports of community programs being established to teach adult parenting skills to older persons with adult children (Creighton, 1993).

Studies suggest that differences in mutual parent–child support are more likely associated with social class than with cultural differences. One national survey found that differences in exchanged aid between whites and Mexican-Americans were related to life-course differences (i.e., availability of kin and family size). Blacks were linked to low income groups in reporting less intergenerational giving than other ethnic groups (Eggebeen & Hogan, 1990). This association was corroborated in another study that coupled this finding with lower educational attainment of black mothers, who, more often than white mothers, are household heads (Goldscheider & Goldscheider, 1991). Whether or not adult children are relatively well off, since most of them do eventually fly the coop, parent–child and couple relations do need to be reconsidered.

For children reaching adulthood in the latter half of the twentieth century, the departure from the parental home has less to do with being economically independent than with being free from parental authority (Burch, 1981). This freedom can be expressed in the child's sense of self-efficacy. Research that surveyed 253 undergraduates attending a Midwestern U.S. university found that students who recalled their parents as being emotionally responsive to their needs were more likely to show high levels of self-efficacy (Mallinckrodt, 1992).

In the negotiated movement toward autonomy, neither the children nor their parents may anticipate again living under the same roof. For some families, however, the situation is different. Adult children may remain living with their parents long after the children's age mates have left their parents' homes. Alternatively, prodigal sons and daughters may return home after what everyone had expected would be their final departure. Either situation can mean trouble for the marriage and for the parent–child relationship. While conflict should not be presumed, co-residence infringes on the independence of both generations (Ward, Logan, & Spitze, 1992).

In recent years, individuals reaching young adulthood have been part of a large cohort whose members have had to compete for jobs in a less than buoyant economy. Also, many more young adults than in previous decades have attended college. Thus, people of the generation reaching their late teens in the 1980s were more likely, as young adults, to reside with their parents than were people who came of age in the 1960s and 1970s (Glick & Lin, 1986; Boyd & Pryor, 1989). At the same time, the increased occurrence of marital dissolution and unmarried motherhood has also contributed to a rise in the number of adult children returning to the parental home when they needed help (Troll, 1985). One of the most interesting characteristics of the empty-nest period, then, is that it may not be so empty (Matras, 1990; Clemens & Axelson, 1985; Boyd & Pryor,

1989). A child who returns home has been variously referred to as "un-launched" (Aquilino & Supple, 1991) and "incompletely launched" (Schnaiberg & Goldenberg, 1989). Our favorite, though, is the "boomerang" kid (Joe, 1991).

Trying to estimate the rate at which adult children return home is exceedingly difficult. Census data and researchers have typically asked whether there are children residing with parents, not whether they left and then returned. These data are helpful, however, in giving us a sense of what proportion of older parents have adult children residing with them, and also in providing some indication as to whether race or income make a difference in this pattern.

Aquilino (1990) used data from the 1987–88 National Survey of Families and Households in the United States to construct a subsample of 4,893 white, black, and Chicano parents with at least one living child aged 19 or over. Using these data, he found, not surprisingly, that the youngest parents (44 years or less) were most likely to have children at home (41%) (Aquilino, 1990, p. 417). However, parents aged 55 to 64 were, by virtue of their age, the most likely to have young adult children.

More than a quarter of these respondents (28%) reported co-resident children. For parents aged 65 and older, the proportion reporting co-resident children dropped to 14%.

In Canada, similar figures are available for children from Statistics Canada. All of the available literature suggests that in the 1980s the cohort aged 20 to 29 showed the biggest increase in co-residency (Ubellacker, 1993; Canadian Press, December 1992). Boyd & Pryor (1989, p. 467) note that between 1981 and 1986 co-residency increased from 60.4% to 63.8% among single females 20 to 24 years of age and from 66.2% to 69.2% for single males in this cohort. Among those 25 to 29 years of age, co-residency for both sexes was about half that of the younger cohort but showed a similar increase between 1981 and 1986: 32.3% to 35.8% for women and 41.0% to 44.8% for men. In contrast, during the 1970s the 20 to 29 age group showed declining co-residency (Boyd & Pryor, 1989).

With respect to the influence of educational level and race on co-residency, Aquilino's (1990) results showed evidence that education and race can easily be confounded. Well-educated sample members, in general, had higher numbers of unmarried co-resident children than did the overall sample. Among the subsample of African-Americans, there also were more co-resident unmarried children than in the overall sample. This is a function of marital status among the children and not cultural differences. Young adult African-Americans are more likely to be single than are their white counterparts. Among well-educated African-Americans, however, the Anglo/African co-residency pattern was reversed: Well-educated African-Americans were more likely than the overall sample to live independently prior to marriage (Aquilino, 1990, p. 412). Therefore, generally, evidence did not support the "cultural preference argument" (Aquilino, 1990, p. 418). Only Mexican-American parents were significantly more likely than other respondents to have a co-resident child.

Canadian data on social background and ethnicity suggest that each makes a difference in co-residency. Adult children were more likely to reside with their parents if they lived in large metropolitan areas; had Greek, Portuguese, Italian, or French as their mother tongue; had less than a high school education; were full-time students; and had a low income. Stepchildren were less likely to co-reside. Children were also less likely to co-reside when parents were separated or divorced, especially when it involved living with a single father (Boyd & Pryor, 1989, pp. 474–475).

The statistics on co-resident children include both those who have not left home and those who have returned. While we can't separate the "haven't left" from the "Hi, I'm back" group, it does appear clear that young adults are more likely now to reside with parents than they have been over the past 20 years. These recent increases in the rates of co-residency among those 20 to 29 have important implications. Living together creates a situation where each generation can have some control over the behavior of the other. As Boyd and Pryor (1989, p. 475) point out, "reciprocal intergenerational monitoring" is likely to occur: Parents monitor, and evaluate, their adult children's behavior; and the children, in turn, monitor and evaluate that of their parents. As a consequence, the behavior of both may change. For example, in a household comprised of a widowed mother and her divorced daughter, each may influence the choice of an appropriate dating partner for the other.

A large national study (Aquilino & Supple, 1991) and a survey of 677 Boston households (Suitor & Pillemer, 1987) each found that the presence or absence of conflict between parents and co-residing adult children was the best predictor variable of relations between the parents. Children's being financially dependent or unemployed, and separated or divorced with accompanying grandchildren, contributed to a decline in parental satisfaction regarding co-residency (Aquilino & Supple, 1991). These findings are supported by another study, consisting of middle-income, primarily Anglo respondents (Ward, Logan, & Spitze, 1992). These researchers note that it is child characteristics and not parental ones that are predictive of satisfaction with co-residency. However, their data reflect only the parents' perceptions. When the authors report that higher income parents are less likely to have co-resident children than are lower income parents, their interpretation is that the children of high income parents are less likely to need co-residency (Ward, Logan, & Spitze, 1992, p. 220). Knowledge of the children's point of view could provide alternative explanations.

Because co-residency typically occurs when children need renewed support, parents are generally willing to give it a try as long as they are financially able. The fact that certain child financial and marital status characteristics increase the likelihood of conflict does not mean that co-residency does not work; indeed, generally such relationships are quite sound. A study involving 372 families that looked for sources of parent–child conflict found that generally relations were good when children "boomeranged" home (Suitor & Pillemer, 1988). The extent to which "boomerang" children have a negative impact on spousal relations depends in part on family relations dating back to when the children were young.

If parents have to reassume responsibility for their children's welfare, they are that much less able to fulfill their own ambitions (Clemens & Axelson, 1985). The degree of disruption in the lives of the parents depends on the age, health, and social circumstances of both generations (Shanas & Sussman, 1981). Parents in late middle age, for example, might have very ambitious plans that the return of children could seriously disrupt (Clemens & Axelson, 1985). Older parents who are still healthy, but less active, might be able to take on renewed parenting responsibilities without feeling resentment. If, however, the parents are not well, then the adult child's need for assistance can create distress for everyone. Neither generation may be able to provide the desired help to the other.

An example of this problem occurred recently in one of our families. Joan Norris and her sister were saddened that neither their mother nor their respective mothers-in-law were available to help when they came home with newborns. The parents, who were not well, were able to help indirectly with money to buy the assistance they could not offer directly. The daughters appreciated this and continued to lend a hand with their ailing mother, but not to the extent they would have had they not been tied down with young children.

In addition to coping with needy children, and possibly grand-children, older parents may have to adjust to a loss of intimates who die or move away upon retirement. Further responsibilities are added when *their* parents become frail, and caregiving becomes necessary. If the range of empty-nest life events clash rather than complement each other, this can strain relations between grandparents, children, and grandchildren. The complications that can arise may be quite serious (Clemens & Axelson, 1985).

Intergenerational Reciprocity

When children return home, or stay at home too long, parents are likely to feel resentment as well as guilt. They want to do everything they can for their children while still protecting time for themselves and their marital relationship (Clemens & Axelson, 1985). The ensuing tension can lead children to revert to their predeparture status and behavior, at the same time as parents rediscover their overriding parental authority. Nevertheless, even though a child's return might well cause tension, it is also likely that both parent and child can accept the return because, whatever difficulties it may bring, it is still better than any alternative arrangement (Glick & Lin, 1986).

Children want to be independent and will normally seek reciprocity when asking for aid from parents. Parents will normally also seek reciprocity in order not to see children as a continuing burden. Reciprocity, the sense of an equitable exchange (Gouldner, 1967), is important for the dignity of all persons concerned. Establishing and maintaining a balanced, reciprocal exchange requires negotiations across the life span (Hagestad, 1981).

The search for reciprocity is made more complex by the fact that a mother and father may not experience the exchange in the same way. For example, when a child is in distress because of divorce or addiction, it is the mother who most directly feels stress. Fathers are distressed to the extent their wives are, and so respond to their child's situation more indirectly (Greenberg & Becker, 1988).

Equity and reciprocity between parents and children is realized in the overall relationship and not in any one episode. Many occasions and events across the family's life cycle contribute to a feeling of equity among its members (Lerner et al., 1988).

Imbalances, when they occur, can leave either the parents or their children in a condition of relative dependence. This is true despite the fact that some researchers believe that children have an obligation to their parents that cannot be redeemed, regardless of the effort made by the child (Berman, 1987). While it is true that no child ever cares for a parent to the degree and over the same length of time that the parent cared for the child, this is not necessarily a source of never-ending guilt for all children. Neither is it impossible for children caring for a chronically ill parent to exhaust themselves to the same extent that their parents did for them.

Conclusions and Summary

In this chapter, we have seen that it is misleading to think that when children leave home they have "grown up" and no longer need their parents. Young adult children are only semiautonomous when they move out of the nest. Moving out is part of the process of negotiating that autonomy.

Parents do have more time and money when children leave home. It is a time when their relationship with each other changes, if for no other reason than that the children have moved out. In consequence, they come face-to-face with each other's individual and couple needs in a way they have not done since becoming parents. Nevertheless, children do go home again, figuratively or in fact, and when they do it is because they need their parents. Older parents, then, must restructure their relationship with each other at the same time as their relationship with their children continues to develop too. "Intimacy at a distance" between parents and children has different meanings in different family and cultural settings. Each family has to communicate with each other to determine what kind of separateness and closeness is appropriate for them. They make this determination in a give-and-take relationship involving multiple generations.

This means that when parents negotiate their way through the not-so-empty-nest period, the circumstances are complex. Having more time and money to enjoy with a spouse is only an older adult's first impression of this time. The second and more enduring impression is that he or she is not free of the demands of children.

Autonomy norms and desires for "intimacy at a distance" notwithstanding, economic recession and high divorce rates in recent years have meant that the norm of independence has been challenged by adult children's increasingly common returns to and delayed departures from the parental home. Resenting these ongoing demands yet wanting to do all that can be done for semiautonomous children presents a dilemma for parents that is perhaps never solved, merely managed. If this sounds discouraging, is it any more difficult than anything parents have known before? In all likelihood, it is just the latest in a series of developmental periods in the family life cycle when couples are faced with the choice of "sink or swim." Most families recognize the lack of a realistic alternative and swim without ever consciously choosing to do so.

Global reciprocity and attachment are evident in these situations. Unbalanced exchanges are taken in stride because each generation knows that equity, sustained by attachment, is long term and not situational.

As the literature suggests, most couples appear to manage quite well. And the research literature is probably quite correct, even though much of it considers marital relations in the empty-nest period *outside* of the context of ongoing parenting. Not only does parenting continue, but the parenting role at this time often takes on the additional task of grand-parenting. In the next chapter we consider the ways in which grandparenting can either enrich or enslave older couples.

4 Grandparenting As Give and Take

GRANDFATHER: I think that when you become a grandparent the kids, your children, become closer to you than if they didn't have any children. One reason is that if they don't have children they have no ties and so they are on their own and away so much. With children, they are more or less tied down and they settle down and I think that they go back to their parents. And so in that respect I guess being a grandparent, then your children usually come back.

GRANDMOTHER: I think too that then you have something in common.

GRANDFATHER: Yes they've got some responsibility now and so they slow down I guess and come back to their parents. Hey Mom, hey Dad, have you got this, can I have some of that?

INTERVIEWER: So you think that is a nice cycle that you go through when they come back?

GRANDFATHER: Oh yes. When you haven't got any married children they disappear more or less because they have other interests and so they are not interested in their parents for a time. And so when they get married it's the same until they have their own friends and then when the children come along, that's when they come back to the parents because they have something in common.

(61-year-old grandfather and 51-year-old grandmother of four;
Norris & Tari, 1985)

59

Compared with couples living in the early 1900s, couples today become grandparents at an earlier age, typically in their later 40s and early 50s (Gee, 1991). Because of this and also because they live longer, they remain in the role longer—being grandparents for perhaps three or four decades (Barranti, 1985).

Recent shifts in fertility patterns towards mothers who are older at the birth of their first child (Hagestad, 1981) could give the impression that such an extended period of grandparenting is becoming unusual. It is likely, however, that such an impression would be incorrect. Data from Statistics Canada, for example, indicate that the median age of all women bearing children in a given year has increased from 25.4 years in 1971 to 28.1 years in 1990 ("Canada's birth rate," 1992). However, birth rate figures suggest that this pattern reflects baby boom children waiting longer to have their children and then beginning and completing their childbearing in a very compressed period of slightly more than two years (Gee & Kimball, 1987). Birth rates, which had been falling steadily after the baby boom, began to rise in 1987; between 1988 and 1990 the Canadian crude birth rate increased slightly, from 14.4 to 15.3 live births for every 1,000 Canadian women of childbearing years. Statistics Canada crude birth rate figures for 1991, however, have dropped below 15, suggesting the baby boomers have essentially completed their childbearing.

Thus, the recent delay in childbearing—like the blip in the crude birth rates—is simply a baby boom aftershock. Given the anomalous character of the baby boom, it is not too surprising that demographers failed to anticipate the blip (Settles, 1987). The net effect of this relatively brief aftershock of older first time mothers is a negligible diminution of the grandparenting part of the life cycle. Relative to generations from the turn of the century, then, women—who still marry young—live longer and extend grandparenthood.

In the previous chapters, we have discussed the interrelationship of members of one generation, the marital couple, and then of two generations, the couple and their children. In this chapter, we will examine the dynamics of the three-generational family, whose members include the original couple, their adult children, and their grandchildren. Support and assistance within such a multigenerational context will be considered by focusing on the situation of the grandparents. Four broad questions will be addressed: How is the transition to grandparenthood anticipated and then made? What is the meaning of this new role? How does the older couple negotiate an exchange relationship involving two younger generations? What are the most frequent trouble spots encountered as a result of grandparenting? Once again, these issues will be considered within the context of family attachments throughout the life course. Wherever the literature exists, we will note the effect of variations in family structure and ethnicity upon the grandparenting experience.

The Pregrandparental Period

For parents who have had children "on-time," late middle age may bring both more freedom and added responsibilities. It is likely to be an extremely busy period. Adult children have left home (perhaps more than once!) and become independent, establishing friendships, careers, and marriages of their own. In response to this, parents may become somewhat distant from their children, enjoying the empty nest and involving themselves with peers and new interests (Norris, 1986). For many, however, this newfound freedom is tempered by added caregiving responsibilities for their own aged parents. This role may demand a large expenditure of personal resources such as time, money, and emotional support.

Perhaps because this period is so busy, parents are not likely to lobby to become grandparents, whatever popular wisdom and the media suggest (Fischer, 1986). Nevertheless, research does indicate that parents of married children think about what it might be like to have grandchildren (Cunningham-Burley, 1986). At the funeral of Joan Norris's grandmother, her youngest uncle—the father of three currently childless young adults—speculated about the meaning of grandparenthood. Looking at his great-niece Sarah, Joan's daughter, he mused that he would probably feel about grandchildren the way he felt about Sarah. He would appreciate the special qualities of each one, yet enjoy the fact that they would go home at the end of the day! In making such an observation, this middle-aged man was anticipating the feelings of those already grandparents: Grandchildren provide pleasure without the responsibilities of parenting (Norris, 1986).

The Transition to Grandparenthood

In the movie *Terms of Endearment*, a mother is shocked and horrified at her married daughter's announcement that she is pregnant. The mother makes it clear that becoming a grandmother signifies her old age, and she has no desire to be a senior citizen just yet. Is this a common reaction when prospective grandparents first receive the news? There has been very little written about the transition to grandparenthood, so the answer to this question is unclear. Certainly, some couples may feel odd, or even resentful, that they had no control over an event that presented them with a new role and new responsibilities (Hagestad & Lang, 1986). Margaret Mead (1972), in her autobiography *Blackberry Winter: A Memoir,* described such feelings when she spoke of the strangeness of being "transformed not by any act of one's own but by the act of one's child" (p. 302).

Also, some parents who had difficulty raising their own children, or who do not relate well to the very young, may be apprehensive about the grandparenting role. One can well imagine that this 62-year-old grandmother may have been less than enthusiastic about her new role. She is certainly clear about how difficult she finds being a grandparent asked to look after an infant grandchild:

We are supposed to feel that mothering is a great mission and ga-ga about grandchildren and a wallet full of pictures and boring everyone who will listen to us about their sweet little expressions . . . . That two weeks [my baby granddaughter] was here was the hardest thing I have ever done in my life. I was standing on the verandah waiting for [my daughter-in-law's] cab to pull up the day she came to pick her up . . . . I look forward to the day when my granddaughter is a teenager and I can do things with her. I think I will love it. I think I have a special feeling for that age.   **(Norris & Tari, 1985)**

The available literature suggests that most grandparents have less trouble with the transition to grandparenthood than did this woman. When problems do arise, they appear to be due to timing. A recent study noted that most Canadian women who become grandmothers do so in late middle age (i.e., on average at 50.4 years) and state that this is the "right" time for the transition (Gee, 1991). Very early, "off-time," grandparenthood, due, for example, to an unplanned teenage pregnancy, can be very distressing. Grandmothers in this situation typically have less time to prepare for the event and may find it difficult to imagine themselves involved with the grandchild (McGreal, 1983). Some may actively reject their new role, transferring it instead to a great-grandmother who may then feel overburdened herself (Burton & Bengtson, 1985). Thus, typical patterns of intergenerational attachment and close, identity relationships become disrupted.

Conflicts in timing with other significant life events experienced by the older couple can also interfere with the development of a grandparental relationship. One researcher, Troll (1985), illustrated this by comparing her own personal experience with that of her sister, a homemaker. "My first year as a grandmother was spent revising my dissertation and learning how to be a college teacher. Her first year was spent sewing baby clothes, writing letters to her daughter—the baby's mother—and waiting for new photographs" (p. 138). In Troll's case, continuing her education in middle age interfered with active involvement as a grandparent.

Other events such as remarriage and parenting a second family can also make the transition to grandparenthood difficult or unwelcome (Hagestad & Lang, 1986). Even more difficult for older couples can be the onset of "reparenting": parenting grandchildren in the absence of one's adult children (Larsen, 1990/1991). Because this situation occurs when the parents have been neglectful or have died, both grandparents and grandchildren are likely to have trouble adjusting. The children miss their parents or may carry the scars of abuse; the grandparents could find all of their resources severely stressed and may worry that they will repeat the parenting mistakes they believe to have caused their own children's incompetence as parents (Larsen, 1990/1991). Nevertheless, the attachment grandparents feel toward their children and grandchildren is likely to keep them in this situation, regardless of the costs. Also, recent legislation dictating that the "least intrusive" changes be made to children's lives when they come into care (Thomlison & Foote, 1991) ensures that grandparents will continue to be asked to support them.

When couples are not propelled into situations such as reparenting and perceive the timing of grandparenthood to be right, the transition can be a smooth and positive experience for older couples. As the interview opening this chapter suggests, adult offspring may rediscover and appreciate their parents when they have children of their own. Daughters and their mothers, in particular, actively negotiate new roles and patterns of aid and support (Fischer, 1981). Such involvement appears to reinforce the two older generations' attachment to each other, and to extend this attachment to the new generation, the grandchildren. As Kivnick (1988) notes, renewed involvement in parenting gives the older couple an opportunity to experience "grandgenerativity," a sense of biological renewal and commitment to their family's future:

Well, when I first knew I was going to be a grandmother, it was like the doctor telling me that I was pregnant only I didn't have to go through 9 months carrying the child or the pain of having it. I watched with anticipation for the day that she would arrive. I went to the hospital as soon as I could to see it and I was just so thrilled. It gives your life a different dimension when you have grandchildren. There is added love and they bring in fresh thoughts and fresh things all the time.   (65-year-old grandmother; Norris & Tari, 1985)

The Meaning of Grandparenthood

Many writers have commented that the grandparent role is an ambiguous one (Denham & Smith, 1989; Sanders & Trygstad, 1989). Even longtime grandparents may not be quite clear about what is expected of them, a situation that has created a wave of recent "how-to" books, periodicals, and films (Denham & Smith, 1989, review some of these). Researchers have attempted to address this ambiguity by exploring the perceived meaning of grandparenthood to grandparents themselves. The apparent goal has been to distill these perceptions into a typology that would generalize to the experiences of all grandparents.

The earliest study in this vein was carried out by Neugarten and Weinstein in 1964. From their data, they identified five styles of grandparental interaction—formal, funseeker, surrogate parent, reservoir of family wisdom, distant figure—and five categories of significance—biological renewal, emotional self-fulfillment, teacher, vicarious achievement, remote. Most subsequent studies did not try to replicate this work but to develop new typologies instead. For example, Robertson (1977) identified four grandparental role types: apportioned, remote, individualized, symbolic. Kivnick (1981) found five others: centrality, valued elder, immortality through clan, reinvolvement with personal past, indulgence. Rather than clarify the meaning of grandparenthood, these efforts, then, have added to the confusion (Norris, 1986).

Why has there been so little consistency in terminology among studies of grandparenting? One obvious problem is that it is difficult to categorize the experiences of such a diverse group of people. Grandparents range from their late 20s (in a family characterized by teenage parenthood) to their 90s (when grandparents may also be great- or great-great-grandparents). They have different life experiences, genders, and ethnic or cultural backgrounds. With the exception of gender, researchers have not investigated in any systematic way the influence of these variables. A recent book summarizing the available research on aging and ethnicity, for example, lacks even a "grandparenting" entry in the index (Driedger & Chappell, 1987).

An equally important problem in the grandparenting literature is how researchers have interpreted their findings. Essentially similar data have been categorized in different ways by different researchers. Very little attention has been given to theoretical grounding. Because theory-driven research poses questions about general concepts and processes, rather than searching for discrete, one-time phenomena, it may permit common global patterns and explanations to emerge.

For example, one study examined the importance of grandparenting within the context of other familial and nonfamilial life events, rather than as a role change unconnected to the other family roles grandparents occupy (Norris, 1986; Norris & Tari, 1985). Taking an inductive approach to their data, the authors proposed that couples whose children have recently been launched may engage in a period of psychosocial moratorium during which they sort out new priorities and interests (Norris & Tari, 1985). This moratorium period is considered similar to the one that occurs during late adolescence as various adult lifestyles are considered. If grandparenthood occurs during this time, attachment to grandchildren may be less intense than if the transition had occurred earlier, before the moratorium, or later, after it has been resolved and grandparents have an established lifestyle once more. The moratorium concept provides a means of explaining grandparenthood within a life-span context, as well as an avenue for future research.

In view of the lack of such theory-driven research, readers must decide for themselves the usefulness of the competing typologies of the grandparenting experience. At the very least these data, derived from categories of experience but not integrated by any conceptual framework, may have value in that they point to concerns and issues raised by older couples in a variety of contexts. Some older couples may never find grandparenting to be an important part of their lives. Nevertheless, it appears that some grandparents who feel remote from their grandchildren still value the role and feel positive about it (Doka & Mertz,

1988). This may be partly because they can anticipate a time when they will feel closer to their grandchildren—for example, when they have retired, grown older, or live in closer proximity. Thus, remoteness can be seen as one phase of the grandparenting experience, rather than as a stable personality characteristic. The 64-year-old grandfather quoted below finds it hard to deal with babies; if both his grandchildren were at this stage, he would certainly be typed as remote. When his feelings about his older grandson are explored, however, it is clear that he is capable of warmth, support, and pride. His role as grandfather should also achieve greater importance as his infant granddaughter matures:

[Grandchildren] are nice when they are little to play with and take pictures of them, but one thing I think is true is the saying that it's nice to have the grandchildren around because you can get rid of them. That's true, that's true. We were over at my daughter's house the other night and the baby was crying and I don't like holding little babies. When they get older that's fine but I don't like walking the floor with crying kids . . . . My grandson's age is better where you can play with them and feed them ice cream and spoil them. (Shows a picture to interviewer.) This is my grandson, who I am quite proud of. He is a nice boy, a good boy.

(grandfather of two; Norris & Tari, 1985)

The Couple as Grandparents

As with other transitions encountered by a husband and wife, successful adjustment to grandparenthood requires communication and negotiation. This, however, is not reflected in the literature. Most research on grandparenting focuses on individual grandparents and does not consider what the experience is like for the *couple*. Because the role is significant for most grandparents, it is likely that there will be issues of concern and uncertainty that must be discussed and managed. Many of these issues are related to gender and sex role differences between grandmother and grandfather.

Grandfathers feel that the focus should be on instrumental assistance (Hagestad, 1985). They are most comfortable engaging in "men" talk (getting a job, managing money) with their grandsons. Women are typically in charge of "family business" (Fischer, 1988). Thus, it is not surprising that grandmothers have well-developed views on what makes for successful grandparenting. Relative to their husbands, wives feel that it is more important to be physically close to their grandchildren and have the opportunity for daily involvement (McGreal, 1983). They also feel it is important to provide their grandchildren with both interpersonal and instrumental support. Grandmothers are ready to address concerns related to family relations and friendships, as well as the practical matters of everyday life, and do so both with their grandsons and their granddaughters (Hagestad, 1985). This interest in grandchildren can take on parental overtones in multigenerational households, particularly when supported by family norms: for example, in single-parent black families (Wilson, 1989).

The interest that grandmothers have in family matters gives the role a "matrifocal tilt" (Hagestad, 1985): Continuity down through the generations in a family is maintained by the oldest women. Thus, the closest intergenerational relationships tend to involve the maternal grandmother and her daughters and granddaughters. Paternal grandparents, particularly grandfathers, may feel less sure of their role and less close to their grandchildren (Fischer, 1988; Kennedy, 1990). When family relationships are strained, as in the case of divorce, paternal grandparents find themselves even further distanced from their grandchildren (Gladstone, 1989).

Given the influence of gender on grandparenting relations, it is likely that husband and wife will occasionally be at odds with one another over the extent and type of contact sought with grandchildren. If a grandmother feels that year-round contact with her grandchildren is essential to good family relationships, but her husband feels that six months in Florida is at least as important, there may be tension. Similarly, a problem exists when a grandfather believes that his wife should provide full-time baby-sitting for their daughter, but this grandmother wants to reenter the work force in another way. Issues such as this require the partners to clarify their position and negotiate a solution. As we have noted elsewhere in this book, good communication is vital to couples experiencing family life cycle changes.

Helping in Multigenerational Situations

Grandparents Helping Their Children and Grandchildren

The literature suggests that adult children find the relations among themselves, the grandparents, and the grandchildren challenging as well.

The metaphors used in this research suggest conflict, if not outright warfare: Grandparents are considered to be the "family national guard" (Hagestad, 1985) or "watchdogs" (Troll, 1985), ensuring the continuity of the family and protecting its values. Within this framework the older couple becomes part of some senior citizen's security service with whom it is safest to communicate only in "demilitarized zones" (Hagestad, 1981)!

But is there really evidence of such problematic, or suspicious, relationships among the generations? On the basis of 1000 interviews with grandparents, a psychiatrist, Kornhaber (1985), suggests that there is. Indeed, he has argued for the "existence of a powerful counterveiling force which vitiates the instinct to grandparent, and with that instinct, the primordial bond between grandparents and grandchildren" (Kornhaber & Woodward, 1981). He places the blame for this evil force squarely on the shoulders of the middle generation, the parents. Instead of maintaining a "lineage bridge" from grandparent to grandchild, adult children have apparently — to continue the military metaphor—blown it up.

Nevertheless, there are data to suggest that parents do influence the grandparenting role (Robertson, 1975). Adult children want to preserve strong attachments to their parents and desire to foster attachment between grandparent and grandchild (Thomas, 1990). They also value the grandparents' ability to relate their life experience, uphold traditions, and provide stability to the family (Thomas, 1990). As the comments of this 65-year-old grandmother confirm, such values are quite consistent with those of grandparents themselves:

The family knows that I always serve Sunday dinner in the dining room . . . and when we have supper here, the girls will come in and they are dressed in a dress and they are not allowed to run around like crazy on Sunday. Sunday is Sunday and it has to be different than the rest of the week. That's just me and something that is tradition in our house.   **(Norris & Tari, 1985)**

From the parents' point of view, the highs and lows of the grandparenting experience are often a result of the kind and amount of intergenerational assistance requested and received. Thomas's (1990) study, for example, noted that middle-aged mothers value grandparents most for their "help." Other research has indicated that parents expect tangible assistance with their children when necessary (Aldous, 1985). Parents also seem receptive to intangible support such as advice on parenting (Tomlin & Passman, 1991). Indeed, when grandparents are missing or unavailable, adult children feel keenly the absence of someone to provide child-rearing tips. The response of one California hospital to this problem has been the establishment of a "warm line" to provide advice, over the telephone, to new parents from an experienced grand-mother of six (Carter, 1990).

In spite of this apparent need for help with child rearing, there appear to be feelings of ambivalence attached to actual acceptance of advice from grandparents. The very limited evidence available suggests that cultural and ethnic variables have a strong influence on these feelings. For example, in some African-American families with a history of single parenting by mothers, advice and tangible help from older generations is a strong family norm (Wilkinson, 1987). Similarly, in traditional Asian families, guidance from grandparents, who are likely to be co-residents, is expected (Osako, 1976). On the other hand, white, middle-class mothers hold strongly negative attitudes about "interference" in their child-rearing activities (Kennedy, 1990; Thomas, 1990), causing the "warm line" grandmother herself to warn new grandparents never to offer unsolicited advice (Carter, 1990).

Concerns about interference are felt acutely by older couples. To a great extent, they follow the lead of their children. Grandparents do not want to be seen as meddlesome, nor do they want to provide support to their children's family on a regular basis (Aldous, 1985). When asked, for example, if they would consider providing full-time child care for their grandchildren, only 2 of 35 grandparents in one recent study replied that they would (Norris, 1986; Norris & Tari, 1985). The remainder indicated that they lacked the personal resources or the desire to do so. Once again, it should be noted that these feelings may reflect those of the dominant culture. A study by Tari (1983) found that a group of Hungarian-born grandparents were happy providing live-in care for their Canadian grandchildren.

Regardless of their cultural background, older couples seem aware that part of their role is to provide help, even when they might not want to. Nevertheless, contradictions between what children say they want (i.e., tangible help) and what they actually want (no interference) could place grandparents in a "double bind," making it impossible to do the "right" thing (Thomas, 1990). Older couples deal with this problem by making it clear that they will provide assistance in an emergency but not on a continuing basis. As one 68-year-old grandfather observed:

First the parents should look after their children, and the children should have all the support from their own parents. If there is a problem or support is not adequate, then I think that a grandparent should step in, but I don't think a grandparent should meddle with their children . . . . Decisions about the grandchildren should come from the parents, but the grandparents should just be overseeing and if something goes wrong then maybe step in, but not be the driving force. **(Norris & Tari, 1985)**

Other research indicates that older couples do make good on their offers of assistance during difficult times. Studies of divorce, for example, indicate that contact between grandparents and an adult child with children may increase after a marital breakdown (Gladstone, 1988). In such circumstances, the older couple typically provides a whole range of assistance: moral support, help with household chores and maintenance, baby-sitting, and gifts or loans of money (Aldous, 1985). Consistent with their belief that such help is temporary, however, grandparents withdraw the help once a child's circumstances improve: for example, upon remarriage (Aldous, 1985).

As we noted in Chapter 1, young families may also receive financial assistance for major purchases such as a house or car. Early in their marriage, the older couple probably were helped by their own parents. Now, as grandparents, they seem ready to assist their children, even though they themselves have experienced the tension that family loans often bring to intergenerational relationships. Perhaps one reason older couples are willing to take such risks is to maximize support for their adult children: Grandparents are likely to live long past the time when their children are establishing their adult lives and could benefit most from an inheritance. Thus, loans and gifts become substitutes (Settles, 1987).

Adult Children and Grandchildren Helping Grandparents

Is the help grandparents provide for their adult children and grandchildren reciprocated? According to the research, families give little tangible aid to healthy, young, and well-off grandparents. Instead, affection and attention are expected by the grandparents (Barranti, 1985). These are critical factors in maintaining parent–child attachment and the commitment to future help, should it be needed (Cicirelli, 1983b). Grandparents seem to take the long view, helping the younger generations whenever necessary and "banking" this help for their own future needs (Ingersoll-Dayton & Antonucci, 1988).

The extensive literature on caregiving provided to frail parents by their children suggests that this approach is quite effective. Older adults are well supported by family members, who often provide care at significant personal expense to themselves (Brody, 1985). Despite media reports of the overburdened and "sandwiched" middle-aged daughter (Underwood & DeMont, 1991; Zwarun, 1991), however, most families seem to accept this responsibility and take it in stride (Lewis, 1990). This is particularly the case when intergenerational relationships are characterized by healthy emotional closeness and flexibility (Norris & Forbes, 1987) as well as the belief that caregiving supplies rewards as well as costs (Walker & Allen, 1991).

There is less information in the available literature on how adult grandchildren might help their grandparents. Some research suggests that grandchildren feel obligated to help if a crisis occurs, and that grandparents expect such help (Robertson, 1976). Nevertheless, there is little evidence that much tangible aid is actually given (Kivett, 1985). It seems likely, then, that under normal circumstances the oldest generation expects some demonstration of love and concern, rather than tangible help (Langer, 1990). Where affection is concerned, apparently, the grandparents are happy to be overbenefited (Langer, 1990). In return, they may provide other kinds of help. It is clear that this 77-year-old great-grandmother, for example, receives attention, affection, and cognitive stimulation in return for the help she gives her great-grandson with his homework:

I've got to finish reading *The Old Man and the Sea* by Hemmingway. It is so interesting. I promised Rob, my 16-year-old great-grandson, that I'd read it and help him put an essay together on it. I feel it is going to be a bit difficult because it has to be put together in a manner I am not familiar with. Will do my best to try and help him. I love to see all my grandchildren.

(Norris, 1978)

What would the situation between this woman and her grandson be if physical or cognitive frailty precluded such interaction? Most of the available literature focuses on the effects of an elder's frailty on the middle generation, not on the grandchildren. One recent study, however, attempted to answer this question by asking young adults to rate their relationship with their "closest" grandparents. Some of these grandparents were in excellent physical and cognitive health, while others were physically disabled or suffered physical and cognitive impairment (Robinson & Stacey-Konnert, 1992). The degree of solidarity that grandchildren felt with their grandparents was heavily influenced by degree of impairment. Cognitive impairment, in particular, was damaging to the relationship. Those who had grandparents with such a disability felt the quality of their relationship had suffered significant declines in the last five years. Nevertheless, regardless of grandchildren's perception of the relationship, all continued to visit regularly, often in situations where there was little apparent reciprocity.

In this study, it appeared that the attachment between grandchildren and grandparents maintained their relationship, despite changes that made it less satisfying. Family norms and obligations probably also operate in such situations, but the power of such norms can also vary depending on the cultural context. Another recent study (Chen, 1992), for example, compared Canadian and Filipino university students' attitudes and affection toward their grandparents. Both groups agreed that they loved their grandparents, felt them to be central members of the family, and noted that they would provide caregiving and financial support when necessary. Nevertheless, Canadian students were much readier to say they would accept co-residence with their grandparents than were Filipino students.

Although it is impossible to determine the reason for this difference from a survey, one might speculate reasonably that many more Filipino than Canadian grandchildren had actually lived with their grandparents, and knew the tensions that could result. Canadian grandchildren were simply endorsing a hypothetical situation that was consistent with the affection they felt for their grandparents. It is likely that intergenerational living would tax their feelings of solidarity as well.

Trouble Spots for Grandparents

Although the research does not provide evidence of widespread conflict in intergenerational relations, there are some situations that can make the grandparenting experience difficult (e.g., Hagestad, 1981; 1985).

Many of these are due to changing family structures or lifestyle decisions made by members of one generation. We will examine several of these trouble spots: timing of grandparenthood, changes in marital status of parents and grandparents, the lifestyles of grandparents, and values clashes between young and old.

Timing

Parents want to become grandparents at an "appropriate" age—for example, late middle or early old age (Troll, 1985). Conflict with children is likely if grandparenthood happens too early, as in the case of teenage pregnancy. Disappointment may be felt if it occurs too late, because, for example, aged grandparents lack the energy or good health for active involvement with grandchildren.

Other timing problems are linked to fertility—both the grandparents' and that of their adult children. Couples producing the baby boom generation, for example, had large numbers of children born over an extended period. This situation increased the probability that the couples would still be parenting dependent children at the same time as they were making the transition to grandparenthood (Gee, 1991). Thus, they may have been less able to assist their adult children than parents of subsequent generations that had children in a shorter period to produce siblings close in age.

Delays in childbearing, infertility, and decisions to remain childless on the part of adult children can also be perceived as timing problems by the oldest generations in a family. The literature on childlessness, however, rarely acknowledges the feelings and influences of potential grandparents, even though as generational stakeholders (Bengtson & Kuypers, 1971), they are likely to be concerned. It would be interesting to discover, for example, how supportive older couples have been of their infertile children's efforts at achieving pregnancy. We know that the children themselves may have difficulty coping both with the procedures and their feelings of being "off-time" for parenthood (Sandelowski, Harris, & Holditch-Davis, 1991; Sandelowski, Holditch-Davis, & Harris, 1990) There is also evidence that they may have difficulty making the transition to parenthood if it does occur, whether through pregnancy or adoption (Daly, 1992; Sandelowski, Holditch-Davis, & Harris, 1992). The support of grandparents in adjusting to this transition could be critical; yet in how-to books on grandparenting these issues are never addressed (e.g., Carter, 1990).

cathy®   **by Cathy Guisewite**

CATHY copyright 1990 Cathy Guisewite.
Reprinted with permission of UNIVERSAL PRESS SYNDICATE.
All rights reserved.

Changes in the Adult Children's Marital Status

A potential problem for grandparenting relationships can come about
when a child's marital status changes. Divorce rates among recently married young adults have increased in recent years. Based on this trend, it is
estimated that a new marriage today may have only a 50–50 chance of
success (Fisher, 1987). With the increasing likelihood that their adult
children will divorce (Gladstone, 1991), there is also the likelihood that
older couples will change the way that they grandparent (e.g., Gladstone,
1987b). Often these changes are unwelcome. When their adult child
does not have custody of the grandchildren, for example, grandparents
may see them less frequently (Matthews & Sprey, 1984). The problem is
made worse when grandparents are in poor health, separated by physical
distance from their grandchildren, or have unresolved conflicts with
their former child-in-law (Johnson, 1985; Gladstone, 1987b).

The strength of the attachment between grandparent and grandchild
is underscored by the pain that forced separation causes:

**Over 2 years is a long time with no contact. I'm afraid the relationship with
Patty will be nonexistent. I feel that I will never see her again. It's like
another death of a loved one.   (grandmother; Gladstone, 1987a)**

Further complications arise when adult divorced children remarry.
On one hand, grandparents may be asked for less help than when their
child was a single parent, and this may provide welcome relief (Aldous,

1985). On the other hand, the new family may bring with it step-grandchildren who must find a place within the multiple generations of the old family. This situation can be trying for an older couple who feel deep attachment to their original grandchildren but little bond to their step-grandchildren (Chilman, 1981). If the adult children demand equal affect and support for all, further strain and conflict can result (Gladstone, 1991).

Changes in the Grandparents' Marital Status

Grandparents themselves may separate or divorce, but the literature, almost hopefully, ignores this issue (e.g., Spanier & Furstenberg, 1987). There is an apparent assumption that all problems within multigenerational families are created by fracturing or blending the families of the middle generation (e.g., Kornhaber, 1985). While divorce is less likely among members of the oldest cohort (Cavanaugh, 1990), many grandparents are considerably younger than members of that generation. Thus, it is possible that grandparents may be in the same situation as their adult children: divorcing their spouses and remarrying others. Over 30% of marriages dissolve after couples have been together for over 15 years (Nett, 1988), and it is likely that many of these couples have both children and grandchildren.

Single grandparenting and the remarriage of grandparents add new complexities to family support. There may be, for example, less time and money available as both grandfather and grandmother establish new households and new relationships. Remarriage may also bring with it stepchildren and step-grandchildren or may result in the addition of newborn children. A 50-year-old remarried father of a new baby, who is also the grandfather of an infant, for example, is not likely to have much time for the grandparent role. A similarly aged remarried mother, bearing children once again with the aid of reproductive technology ("Twins born to California grandmother," 1992), is likely to have even less energy for grandmotherhood. Little is known, however, about how grandparents deal with such competing roles and demands.

A more frequently acknowledged change in the marital status of grandparental couples is that of widowhood (e.g., Martin Matthews, 1991). Immediately after bereavement, widows and widowers may turn to their adult children and to their grandchildren for more support than they asked for previously (Horowitz, 1985). What is the impact of this help-seeking for the grandparenting relationship? Perhaps grandchildren find that they are required to provide more emotional support than they have in the past. One study, for example, found that widows were more likely than other marital status groups to name "other relatives," including grandchildren, as confidants (Strain & Chappell, 1982). This situation is probably temporary, however, as previous levels of reciprocal exchange between parent and child redevelop (Vachon & Stylianos, 1988).

Grandparents' Other Interests

Much of the literature focuses on the grandparental role to the exclusion of older couples' other interests and activities. This research gives the misleading impression that the role has centrality for most older people. Young grandparents, in particular, may be involved in many interests and activities outside the family that leave only restricted amounts of time for grandparenting (Norris, 1986). The comments of these grandparents illustrate the busy schedules of many couples in their 60s:

I am sort of retired, but I have some investment in a little property and I putter around and we have enough money to live reasonably. I do carpentry for friends and I like to be active. I am a director of the Standard Learning Opportunities Group, which is a senior citizens' group . . . and we get visiting professors . . . . I am a director of the tennis club . . . . I am also warden of the Anglican Church.   (62-year-old grandfather; Norris, 1986, p. 61)

My life is extraordinarily busy; my hobbies, well I guess in my old age that the thing I am good at is in games. In my case, golf and bridge. My lifestyle is busy; it's unreal.   (65-year-old grandmother; Norris, 1986, p. 61)

If children and grandchildren do not share the older couple's attitude toward the place of grandparenting within a busy lifestyle, there may be emotional pain, resentment, and conflict. If, for example, children expect their parents to be "on-call" baby-sitters, and the older couple make it clear that they will provide child care only in emergencies (Norris, 1986) or on an occasional basis (Semple, 1985), strained relationships may result. Such problems become compounded when grandparents pursue their interests in geographically remote areas—for example, by becoming snowbirds (Tucker, Marshall, Longino, & Mullins, 1988)—precluding the possibility of providing even emergency family support.

Multiple Generations and Multiple Values

Cohort differences in attitudes toward divorce may make it difficult for grandparents to accept the breakdown of their children's marriages (e.g., Kornhaber, 1985). Other social changes, for example, in gender roles, may be equally unsettling for older couples. For example, this grandfather is clearly uneasy with the fact that both his married daughter and his daughter-in-law are the primary income earners in their families:

Yes, my daughter is more capable than my son. She is more sure of herself; my son is unsure of himself. My son got divorced about 7 years ago and he is married naturally now with a baby coming on. He is very happy right now, but you know parents . . . . My daughter-in-law is making more than my son's wages as far as I'm concerned, which is no concern of mine, but naturally you would like to see your son being kind of the wage earner as far as I'm concerned. And my daughter is making more than her husband is making, as far as that's concerned, which concerns me sometimes too.

(65-year-old grandfather; Norris & Tari, 1985)

The survival of very elderly couples into great-grandparenthood could compound the values clashes within multigenerational families. Some research has suggested, for example, that great-grandparents have difficulty accepting family variations resulting in cohabitation, divorce, and remarriage, or interracial adoption (Doka & Mertz, 1988). Great-grandparents were somewhat distanced from such situations, however, because they happened more often within their grandchildren's families than within their children's families. Thus, a value conflict did not result necessarily in a behavioral conflict within the family.

Conclusions and Summary

As the research suggests, most couples successfully negotiate the transition to grandparenthood and find the role meaningful and satisfying. Grandparents manage to merge this role with other interests and activities, providing help to their adult children's families whenever it is necessary without promising continual support. Their children and grandchildren, in turn, reciprocate with affection, and tangible aid if it is required.

As the conversation that opened this chapter illustrates, husbands and wives typically find that they share the same cohort- and role-based attitudes toward grandparenting. Thus, there is not likely to be a great deal of conflict over decisions related to grandparenting. Nevertheless, there are some sex differences in the approach to grandparenting that may necessitate discussion between husbands and wives. More significantly, there may be differences between generations in expectations for the grandparental role. Once again, conflict may be minimized by strong bonds of attachment among all members of the family, as well as by good communication skill. When changes in family structure further test the grandparental relationship, these qualities become critical.

This chapter organizes the available research on grandparenting around the central theme of this book: how couples negotiate issues of intergenerational support within a context of evolving attachment relations across the family life cycle.

How is the transition to grandparenthood anticipated and then made? The available evidence suggests that grandparents may not spend much energy anticipating grandparenthood unless they perceive the timing to be poor, as when there is a teenage pregnancy. When timing is good, on the other hand, it appears that couples view the role quite positively.

What is the meaning of this new role? There is very little consensus on the specific meaning of grandparenthood to older couples. This is not surprising in view of the many varieties of grandparents. Chronological age, ethnic group membership, and gender may affect the grandparenting experience quite significantly by limiting or encouraging certain types of behaviors. Nevertheless, the stake that grandparents have in the future of their families and the attachment binding them to their children and grandchildren almost always ensure that the role will be an important one. This is true regardless of the circumstances surrounding the transition to grandparenthood and the amount of support older couples provide to the young.

How does the older couple negotiate an exchange relationship involving two younger generations? It is clear from the research that multiple generations of family members do support each other. There is, however, a tension between adult children and grandparents when it comes to help with child rearing. The middle generation values the assistance of the grandparents but may resent overinvolvement. Members of the older generation, on the other hand, may be willing to provide care occasionally or in emergencies, but are unlikely to want to "reparent." Nevertheless, when the situation requires it, because of cultural norms or the unavailability of parents, grandparents regularly take on the role of surrogate parent to the youngest generation.

The literature suggests that unless the older couple is in poor health, support offered for them from adult children or grandchildren is primarily social-emotional. Strong attachment bonds and feelings of filial obligation help to maintain the relationship between young and old regardless of the context.

What are the most frequent trouble spots encountered as a result of grandparenting? Intergenerational dynamics are certain to become more complex with the addition of a new generation. In this chapter, the most common trouble spots for grandparents were discussed. First, timing was considered: Fertility decisions and difficulties on the part of both adult generations can create strain. Second, changes in the marital status of members of either adult generation can produce family variations and conflicting roles. For example, a grandfather and parent of adult children could also be the father of a newborn child and the stepfather of school-aged children. Third, other activities and interests on the part of the grandparental couple could restrict the amount of time, effort, and help available for grandchildren. It is likely, for example, that couples are becoming grandparents when they are still in the work force and may also be parenting dependent children. Finally, differences in values may cause strain between older couples and their children. Beliefs about the changing roles of women, for example, or concerns about equal opportunity for minorities may not be shared by all generations.

In the final analysis, we can say that grandparenthood works because of the continuing attachment and mutual support among all generations. It may be that there are cultural and ethnic differences in the experiences of grandparents and the expectations that others have of them. Certainly, the small amount of research available suggests such variations. Nevertheless, it appears that all grandparents are generational stakeholders. They want to ensure the continuity and happiness of their families, so they usually try to cope with trouble spots. How well they do this depends on good communication between members of the older couple and between generations.

Siblings:
From Rivals to Allies

Uncle Frank is selling his summer cottage, a property that adjoins the cottage owned by Joe Tindale's twice-widowed mother. Uncle Frank's own children have rarely used the cottage since they started their own families and have no interest in buying it. Joe and his siblings, however, are interested because their own family cottage cannot accommodate their mother, four siblings, two step-sibs, and twelve children. They are also interested because Uncle Frank's cottage has sentimental value. He, his brother (Joe's father), and their father built both family cottages. These siblings, nurturing a strong attachment for each other, made it possible for their families to get together in the summer. Now, ownership of the same cottages would enable the next generation, Joe and his siblings, to socialize together each summer. Like their father and mother's generation before them, these sisters and brothers have moved to different cities. Rarely do they and their families have the opportunity to spend time with each other.

There is a stumbling block in the way of buying Uncle Frank's cottage: money. Joe's mother is prepared to make a loan, repayable to her estate, of about one-third of the down-payment. Joe and his siblings would have to put up the rest of the down payment and pay the mortgage and maintenance costs. Joe and his sibs each have substantial financial responsibilities, however, and they find themselves unable to buy this cottage at this time, even in partnership. This seems ironic to them when they consider that their single-earner parents managed on their own.

It is not clear how this situation will turn out. Much will depend on the changing circumstances of each family, as well as the economic context within which financial decisions are made. The story demonstrates the ongoing intergenerational and within-generation negotiations about property and material support that are common in many families. The siblings, uncles, and parents have been trying to make the purchase because these family members share a tremendous sense of attachment. This attachment is part of an integrated whole-family relationship that is continuing to develop.

This chapter considers the nature of attachment among adult siblings within the larger, intergenerational, family context. How and why does such attachment sustain itself? In this book, we discuss family interactions that occur across and between generations. Each of these is uniquely important to the older couple. Gold (1989a), thinking of siblings, makes a point that applies equally well to grandparents and friends. She remarks that "the parent–child, spouse–spouse, and sibling dyads of older people should be viewed as unique and complementary rather than as similar and substitutable" (Gold, 1989a, p. 38).

The study of sibling relationships, once neglected, is rapidly attracting more and more interest (Bedford, 1989a; Chappell, 1991). Initially sibling studies focused on birth order as a predictive variable in the cognitive and social psychological characteristics of individuals (Bedford, 1989b). It was not until the early 1980s that researchers (Bank & Kahn, 1982) legitimized the study of later-life sibling relations when they made it clear that sibling bonds were not limited to child development. Adult sibling relationships have been seen as more important since researchers observed that family support for caregivers correlated with the presence of siblings (Bedford, 1989b). The question now has become, How strongly, and in what manner, do sibling ties continue into old age?

This chapter will explore how, when, and why parents continue to nurture sibling relations at a point in the family life cycle when their children and the grandparents of these children are only precariously autonomous. Children not quite yet on their own continue to return home, literally and figuratively; at the same time, their grandparents are becoming progressively frailer. We will clarify how siblings fit within the attachment literature that frames our analyses and use this understanding to discuss the occurrence and meaning of sibling ties as sources of life-span social support. As we will see, sibling relationships are strongly influenced by demographic and situational variables such as gender, race, and family structure. These factors will also be discussed in the context of the very limited research evidence available.

A Life-Span Conceptualization of Sibling Relationships

Early Interactions

Much of the research on sibling relationships has been carried out within the context of childhood. Researchers agree that brothers and sisters have an important socializing influence upon one another (e.g., Lamb & Sutton-Smith, 1982). In particular, siblings provide companionship, comfort, and affection as well as tangible aid and hands-on care (Goetting, 1986). Typically, this creates a positive context for interaction, but as parents know only too well, fights and rivalry are also important features of sibling relationships in childhood. Friction sometimes results as brothers and sisters employ one another to hone their social skills and compare achievements (McGhee, 1985; Troll, 1975).

Whether interactions among young siblings are harmonious or rivalrous, they emerge from strong bonds of attachment that children develop when raised in the same household. Some researchers have noted that this attachment may become intense enough to create a "conspiracy of silence," a powerful bond of loyalty that excludes parents from some aspects of siblings' lives (Bank & Kahn, 1975). This attachment can be further strengthened by situational factors such as when older siblings provide care for younger brothers and sisters (Goetting, 1986; Weisner & Gallimore, 1977).

As children grow into adolescence and young adulthood and move out of the family home, sibling relationships take on some of the characteristics of friendships; they still provide support, but they become less obligatory and more voluntary (McGhee, 1985). Research suggests that young adult siblings choose to seek out each other's company and support on a regular basis; one study noted that college-aged women perceived that they got as much emotional support from their "closest" sibling as they did from their mother (Cicirelli, 1980a). This suggests that attachment among young adult siblings can be as strong as that between parent and child.

With increasing age, and life events such as marriage and child rearing, the intensity of sibling relationships appears to diminish (Adams, 1968). Couples now devote their "family" time and energy primarily to each other and their children. Siblings may still receive support, but in a more idiosyncratic fashion (Adams, 1968). An occasional loan, gift, or word of advice is given, but not with the same frequency as before. According to Adams (1968), at this period in the family cycle, brothers and sisters are interested in one another but do not rely on one another for assistance or for social comparison to judge their own success; attachment bonds and norms of reciprocal support persevere, but at a low level.

As a number of researchers have noted, the sibling bond typically becomes reactivated in mid-life by declines in older parents' health and independence (Cicirelli, 1980b; Goetting, 1986; Lerner et al., 1991). Siblings are, once again, in relatively frequent contact with each other. Close identity relationships among brothers and sisters may help them weather these caregiving situations, but with some possible cost to the relationship. One group of researchers feels that as personal resources are overtaxed by the demands of frail parents, siblings will begin to feel that they are doing more than their fair share (Lerner et al., 1988). Such perceived inequity can do permanent damage to the sibling bond; "identity" (closely attached) relations may deteriorate to "unit" (unstably attached) or even "nonunit" (no longer attached) relations in which little emotional closeness is felt. The comments below from two sisters illustrate how such deterioration could come about. There are obvious differences in the way that each perceives her contribution to the care of their aged mother:

The burden is all mine except that my sister is coming here to take my mother to visit out-of-state relatives. It would be very nice if someone else were here to help share but they don't and they can't. It's not fair in as much as I have to do everything because they don't live here. If they did, I think they would do more in the way of errands and visiting and I could handle the financial end. That is the way it would be divided. I feel that I'm not meeting all of her needs sufficiently. I need physical help for her and that can't work out because they aren't here.

(the sister who lives in the same community as her mother; Matthews, 1987, p. 434)

My sister thinks we've copped out and taken the easy road in life. And it's not easy to take care of my mother. She's difficult. It's not easy. I'm doing what I can do. My sister knows she can count on me. On the two occasions she called I was on the next plane and I was there. She almost came out and asked me to stay that week after my father died. I've been real careful about professional commitments so I could be flexible and come if I needed to . . . . I worked it out so I let my sister know when I was coming but I never got any feedback . . . . I told her I thought it would give her some free time, but she doesn't really sense that it would matter.

(the sister living far away from her mother; Matthews, 1987, p. 434)

Later-Life Interactions

Increased Salience of Siblings

Researchers have directed much of their recent efforts into investigating how sibling relationships emerge from the competing demands of mid-life into old age (e.g., Cicirelli, 1991). Are old rivalries laid to rest? Do sibling bonds become stronger as other social relationships are lost or diminish in importance? To help answer these questions, it is useful to examine Bedford's (1989b) concept of "incentive value," or increased salience. She hypothesizes that relations between older siblings are characterized by greater salience than existed in the period from childhood through mid-life. The model seeks to explain what might promote increased salience among siblings in later life.

Bedford's data (1989c), from a sample of 71 middle-class persons ranging in age from 20 to 89, suggest that increased salience among siblings in later life occurs not because certain relational components actively increase in significance; instead, these components take on greater salience when sibling conflicts decline. This decline in sibling conflicts often happens passively, as could occur when a sibling became widowed, thereby losing a spouse who may have interfered with a satisfactory sibling relationship. Increased salience could also occur when a retired person moves closer to the family of origin. The opportunity for increased salience among older siblings lies, then, in the absence of obstacles rather than in a reconstruction of the role of siblings in later life.

The increased salience of siblings in later life may be associated with their greater availability as sources of informal support. This appears to be primarily an age, rather than cohort, phenomenon. Regardless of cohort, as one's informal network shrinks through death and migration, siblings' relative availability could well increase. Nevertheless, cohort effects can sometimes interact with these age effects. Some researchers have suggested, for example, that siblings may become more salient for today's generation of young people than they have been for their parents, the baby boomers (e.g., Marcil-Gratton & Legare, 1992). This suggestion has been made because the children of baby boomers have fewer siblings, thereby reducing the pool of potential support. Fewer numbers may heighten salience. Others (i.e., Cicirelli, 1991) agree that a small cohort will make sibling relations more salient for children of baby boomer parents, but also argue that the dependence of baby boomers upon their siblings will grow as they more frequently experience marital breakdown, childlessness, and lifelong singlehood (Connidis, 1989a).

Although they have not examined cohort variations, a number of studies by Gold (1989a, 1989b) have investigated the changing salience of sibling ties with age. In one study, Gold (1989b) considered the "generational solidarity" of siblings, that is, their feelings of affection and extent of contact with one another. Fifty-four individuals over the age of 65 were interviewed about their sibling relationships and then questioned again two years later. Among the dimensions studied, the individuals' perceptions of emotional closeness (affection) and contact did not change. Psychological involvement and feelings of acceptance/approval increased in importance while conflict and feelings of resentment/envy decreased, a finding consistent with Bedford's (1989b) model. From these findings, Gold (1989b, p. 30) argued that emotional support, psychological involvement, and acceptance/approval all contribute to generational solidarity. This construct complements attachment theory and suggests that over the life-span, the sibling bond may be second only to the parent–child bond in importance. In later life, with parents gone, the sibling bond can become the primary attachment.

Later-Life Sibling Typologies

The overall increases in salience of siblings as adults age, however, should not obscure preexisting individual differences in these relationships. The history of interactions among siblings, for example, may have a lasting impact on their relationship in later life (Klagsbrun, 1992). Gold's (1989a) typology of five kinds of sibling relationships—"the Intimate, the Congenial, the Loyal, the Apathetic, and the Hostile" (p. 42)—describes the distinct kinds of sibling dyads that can emerge by later life. These types run on a continuum of emotional closeness: Congenial relations fall just a little short of the full-blown devotion characterized by Intimate sib ties. Those of the Loyal type are characterized by a bond that is not emotionally close, and perhaps most akin to straightforward filial obligation. Apathetic relationships do not express the global reciprocity and affection we expect in attachment relations. They are distant, disconnected, and lacking the passion to generate hostility. Hostile relationships, the polar opposite of Intimate relationships, actively and continually reproduce ongoing grudges.

Discussing Gold's work, Cicirelli (1991, p. 297) acknowledges the value of typologies in organizing qualitative data but argues that this approach can distort the interpretation of data by forcing borderline cases into a type or by over-generalizing from individual cases. We need to realize, for example, that someone may have an intimate relationship with one sibling and experience something quite different with another. Recently, researchers concerned with the "nonshared environment" of siblings have pointed out that although biologically related sibling pairs share 50% of their genes, each person may have a very different experience growing up within the same family (Dunn, 1991; Dunn & Plomin, 1991). An oldest sib, for example, may benefit from the opportunity to teach the youngest sib, who, when he or she reaches the same age, will not have this opportunity. Thus, however useful types are in identifying points on a continuum, it is important to remember that they may be quite situationally and temporally specific.

Despite the limitations of typologies, Gold's work (Gold, 1989a, 1989b; Gold, Woodbury, & George, 1990) offers two important contributions to our understanding of siblings. First, she, along with others mentioned in this chapter, has established the salience of sibling ties in adulthood. Second, her typology was generated from the coding of qualitative-interview transcripts to create seven variables that, combined in various strengths, characterize the types. Psychological involvement is one of those variables, and Gold (1989a, p. 48) cites Cicirelli to remind us that psychological closeness and contact define attachment.

Life-Span Attachment

For his part, Cicirelli (1991, p. 305) makes the point that relationships between older siblings are childhood relations continued through adulthood. Attachment theory provides us with a means of explaining the roots of the ties between siblings and their persistence across the life span. In order for attachment to be nurtured and persist, the attachment figure must be "available and receptive" (Cicirelli, 1989). These requirements can be satisfied without physical proximity or contact. Feelings of attachment between siblings are "satisfied on a symbolic level through the process of identification" (Cicirelli, 1991, p. 305). The psychological closeness that defines attachment thus does not equate with physical contact. An older man makes the point very well in describing how he feels about his sisters:

I pointed out that I had two sisters with whom I have very little in common. And if they weren't my sisters they wouldn't be friends of mine, but the fact that they are my sisters, I am very fond and conscious of them. Whether we see each other or not, I know we love each other and that won't change.

(Norris & Tari, 1985)

Both Gold's (1989a) and Cicirelli's (1989) studies are too limited by small, homogeneous, one-time samples to test the general applicability of attachment theory to the study of siblings. Gold (1989a) studied 60 white, city-dwelling, middle-class adults over the age of 65; Cicirelli (1989) studied 83 men and women of lower-middle-class background living in a small midwestern U.S. city. Nevertheless, Cicirelli (1989) did find support for the use of attachment theory and, like Gold (1989a), found that gender makes a difference. It appears attachment is more likely to characterize sibling ties when sisters are involved (Cicirelli, 1989). He suggests we look further at the importance of gender and use more diverse samples.

Gold similarly found that "it is gender composition of the sibling dyad, rather than the gender of the sibling per se, that influences the type of relationship between brothers and sisters in old age" (1989a, p. 47). Apart from a statistically nonsignificant finding that dyads with a female were more likely to be of the Intimate or Congenial type, and that those with a male more often were characterized as Apathetic, Gold found no clear reason why dyads that included a sister reveal greater psychological closeness. Similarly, Connidis (1989c) found that "despite more frequent contact, sisters appear no more likely than brothers or brother–sister dyads to be close friends or mutual confidants" (p. 91). While confidant may not be synonymous with Intimate, it is clear that the role played by gender in sibling relations is an area for further research.

Class may also play a role. For example, Gold, Woodbury, and George (1990) found that working-class siblings more often provided instrumental support for each other than did middle- or upper-middle-class respondents. Much more needs to be done to establish whether our understanding of attachment among siblings has a white middle-class bias.

While the conceptualization of sibling ties is indeed becoming stronger and more consistent, the research is still largely exploratory. Investigators must acknowledge limitations in sample size and composition, and a near complete absence of longitudinal data. Having said this, there are some appropriate applications of attachment theory to siblings revealed by the available data. Generational solidarity and increased salience do seem to apply and intensify among siblings as they age. Rivalries seem to diminish. Typologies, while inherently limiting, do at least suggest characteristics to look for and track when exploring sibling ties through adulthood. Finally, attachment theory itself is becoming the best explanation of how these various conceptual components complement each other.

Overall, there is sufficient evidence to argue that the attachment theory we have used to characterize relations between parents and their children can be extended to include siblings. Attachment theory has suggested that a need for support among siblings can be satisfied symbolically. Nonetheless, we need some appreciation of how much and what kind of contact occurs between older siblings. We can then ask, as Cicirelli (1991) does, how sibling attachment contributes to well-being among older people generally, and among parental couples specifically.

In a critical review of the literature on sibling relationships in adulthood, Seltzer (1989) noted that data from diverse sources support the conclusion that siblings become emotionally closer and more involved with one another as they age. She also noted, however, that there are many unanswered questions about the effect of variations in the sibling experience on the relationship. In particular, and consistent with our view, Seltzer felt that the effects of ethnicity and cohort have been neglected and that some questions relating to family dynamics have received little attention. To direct researchers toward these issues, Seltzer delineated five areas that could provide a context for future work: the number of sibs and their potential combinations and coalitions, segmentation or partial disclosure in any dyad such that each individual only fully expresses herself or himself in a multiplicity of relations, gender differences in the salience of sibling ties, sibling rivalry, and the impact of a parent's or sibling's death on other siblings (Seltzer, 1989, pp. 112–114). In the next section, we will consider some of these issues within the context of the adult couple's relationship.

Contact among Siblings

In the last five years, the literature on sibling contact in adulthood has grown rapidly. Much of this work has dealt with the extent of contact that brothers and sisters have with one another once they have left the parental home. Too often, however, it does not place empirical questions in a theoretical framework. The result is we have no idea whether the lack or abundance of sibling contact is of any importance to the siblings.

Some psychologists have promoted the idea that sociability, the desire for social contact and the skill to bring about successful interactions, can be linked to the extent of contact with siblings in childhood (see Polit & Falbo, 1987, for a review). It follows that having a large number of brothers and sisters in childhood would produce adults who are more likely to show healthy social functioning than those in small families. One study, however, found no evidence to suggest that the number of siblings had any effect on sociability among adults (Blake, Richardson, & Bhattacharya, 1991). Adults from large families were no warmer, loving, cooperative, or friendly than their peers from small families, nor were they any more likely to engage in mutual support. On the other hand, a recent study of social support and well-being among the widowed and never married suggested that there is a connection between sibling contact and positive mental health. The morale of widows in this study was related positively to the number of siblings with whom they had had face-to-face contact (Martin Matthews, 1991).

It is likely that variations in sample characteristics have a role in producing such conflicting findings. The study by Blake and her colleagues (1991), used existing 1957 and 1976 data sets collected from young couples "purposely free from many reproductive and familial traumas such as multiple miscarriages, stillbirth, child death, divorce and remarriage, and intended separation" (p. 273). The Martin Matthews (1991) study, on the other hand, involved a sample of older adults that included those who had experienced recent bereavement. Husbands and wives who have not experienced extremely stressful life events may have needs for contact and support from extended family that differ greatly from those of people who have endured loss.

The differing chronological ages and birth cohorts represented in these two studies point to another potential source of variation in the sibling research. Baby boomers have more siblings than their parents' generation, and therefore a greater chance of sibling contact (McDaniel, 1986). Although boomers, as a generation, have not yet completed their families, it may be that they also have produced an unusual cohort of siblings. Most baby boom mothers have had their children in a short period, producing siblings closely spaced in age. Recent evidence also points to a dramatic increase in the number of multiple births, the probable result of reproductive technology (Canadian Press, 1993). This cohort phenomenon creates more sibling situations where there is *no* age gap and where siblings are reared together for longer, thus intensifying any effect for contact.

Task-Specific or Compensatory Support?

Variations in family composition make it even more important to consider sibling contact within some overarching theoretical framework. A recent program of research by Connidis (1989a; Connidis & Davies, 1990) illustrates the explanatory power of models of social support in sibling research. The first study found that women previously married, single, or childless have the most active sib ties. In addition to lending further support to the view that gender may make a difference in contact patterns, there is also the suggestion that these individuals have a smaller support system than do married persons with children. Therefore, this research suggests that the provision of instrumental and emotional support by siblings is more important to single adults than to married ones (Connidis, 1989a).

Connidis and Davies (1990) supported this conclusion and also clarified two competing conceptualizations of social support among siblings: the task-specificity and hierarchical compensatory models. Researchers have traditionally applied the compensatory, or substitution, model to older people's social relationships. This model predicts that married parents will turn to children when the spouse is not available, regardless of the kind of support needed. The childless are consigned to a residual category with those who do not have spouses and are assumed to substitute, in a compensatory manner, siblings and friends for these relation-ships. In Connidis's work, however, the task-specificity model, which seeks to identify *types* of supports, was found to be more accurate in describing sibling relations than the traditionally more popular compen-satory model. Task specificity can be operationally defined by a set of relationship characteristics: Siblings are considered either to be com-panions, to have face-to-face contact that is physically close but not necessarily personal, or to be confidants, to have contact that is personal but not necessarily physically close (electronic or written communication can work as well as face-to-face contact).

When tested (Connidis & Davies, 1990), these definitions of task-specific contact brought results consistent with the initial research (Con-nidis, 1989a). The findings indicated that women, especially those single, divorced, or widowed, more often than any other group develop con-fidant ties with siblings. Even so, among those who are married with children, siblings still are considered confidants more often than com-panions. In addition, the choice of confidants and companions by mem-bers of the older couple showed gender differences. This finding suggests that task specificity is at work. Husbands in Connidis and Davies's (1990) research almost universally assigned siblings to a con-fidant rather than companion role; most wives gave sibs both roles.

Motivation for Different Patterns of Sibling Relationships

Looking at task specificity helps us to understand that the different mem-bers in a person's informal network likely fulfill different, if not mutually exclusive, roles. Making sense of contact patterns among siblings can be moved another step ahead if we can shed some light on the motivation for this behavior. In a survey of 400 adult siblings of whom 70% were married and 81% had children, researchers found that analyzing motiva-tions for contact was more fruitful than simply counting contacts (Lee, Mancini, & Maxwell, 1990). Motivations for contact were classified as either obligatory or discretionary. It was found that having children at home did not change discretionary motivation but did relieve the obli-gation to have contact with siblings. This suggests that if they have children, members of a couple who feel an attachment to their brothers and sisters can continue to identify with them, and possibly see them for some task-specific purposes, but may excuse themselves from, for ex-ample, Thanksgiving dinner without any particular guilt.

The following examples from a widowhood study illustrate the differences between obligatory and discretionary motivations for contact (Martin Matthews, 1992). An obligatory relationship is often structured around institutionalized contact. As one elderly widow put it,

We are raised very religious, this is what keeps us together. We are all close through the church.

Another widow put it even more succinctly:

Family ties are more what bring us together rather than common interests.

The following widow distinguishes discretionary contact with her sisters from an obligatory relationship with her brothers.

I never thought of it much. My brothers have different interests—gambling, horse racing, etc. My sisters have more in common with me—we like a good play or an opera. I rely on them a lot for driving me around. For a family celebration we quite often get together—brothers and sisters. Family ties keep me tied to my brothers.

Discretionary sibling relations are simply described by the respondent who reports

I feel very close to my sister. We only have one another and we keep close track of each other.

And then there are the families where even the obligatory motivation has withered:

I don't feel close to my sister *at all*. I value family life and try to keep in contact, but the others don't seem to want to maintain ties—so we don't.

From what has been reported, we know that the members of a mature couple make contact with siblings in a way that is probably task specific, and that seeing a sibling does not necessarily mean that there is inadequate support available from spouse or children. Siblings are also likely to be considered when there is a need for a confidant as opposed to a simple companion. As a result, while mature adults see siblings at obligatory family functions, they also make discretionary choices to make contact when they need to.

The verbatim data of respondents we report here, like the literature generally, reflect predominantly white middle-class views. Cross-cultural data on adult sibling relations are very limited, allowing only speculation about differences in the sibling experience. For example, because a higher proportion of black families than white families are headed by a female single parent (Taylor, Chatters, Tucker, & Lewis, 1990), black children's sibling experiences may differ. One theorist has concluded that older children within single parent families of any ethnic background will be more likely to engage in child care for younger siblings (Goetting, 1986). The attachment developed through such experiences could strengthen lifelong sibling relationships.

A recent study (Taylor et al., 1990) does describe some differences between the kind of help offered by older black siblings and that offered by white siblings, and notes that each group may look for different qualities in their siblings. These results are difficult to interpret, however, because they were obtained outside any theoretical framework. What does it mean that whites will help their sibs with shopping, whereas blacks prefer to provide transportation? Whatever they may mean, these results are not generalizable to other cultural or racial groups. The most we can say is that there are some differences in terms of what motivates sibling contact. More cross-cultural comparisons are badly needed if we are to begin to understand the broad spectrum of people growing older in North American society.

While motivations for contact between siblings vary by marital status, sex, and ethnic background, one unifying observation is that siblings are confidants about whom we make discretionary choices. The question that attachment theory directs us to ask is, What do these sibling interactions do for our well-being? Is there social support provided in knowing that the siblings we feel affection toward are out there, regardless of how and when we actually make contact with them?

Social Support and Closeness among Siblings

On the whole, there are clear indications that siblings do provide social support for each other. Generally, they both give and receive support in a balanced exchange that is reciprocal over the life span. And, as we have seen in earlier chapters, there is a dialectical character to these support systems whereby the attachment among siblings permits long-term reciprocity to take precedence over a need for short-term equity (Avioli, 1989).

Reciprocity and attachment have their roots in the relations siblings have as children and, even more fundamentally, in the relations they have with their families of origin (Pulakos, 1990). In two studies of undergraduate respondents, support within the family of origin and an openness to the expression of feelings were found to predict psychological closeness of siblings as adults rather than the sibling rivalry that, in varying degrees, characterizes sibling relations in childhood (Pulakos, 1987, 1990).

It must be said once again, however, that it is not clear how generalizable such findings are. In an era when nontraditional family forms are becoming commonplace, it is important to remember that individuals may not share researchers' perceptions of their "family of origin." Adopted children and those who have become part of a stepfamily early in their lives may not consider their biological relatives as central to their lives, or even at all part of them. Those conceived through sperm or ovum donation or by surrogate mothers may see their origins as even more complex. Who one's siblings are can be seen to be as much a social construction as a biological reality. Although there is now some limited research on step- and half-siblings (White & Riedmann, 1992), less is known of the developing relationships among adopted siblings (see Rosenberg, 1992, for a general discussion) and nothing is known of sibling relationships among those conceived through reproductive technology.

Family of origin variables are mediated further by aging and life events. For example, the sibling rivalry of childhood is typically overcome by sisters during their young to middle adulthood when they are actively raising children (Bedford, 1989a). In middle age, when their children are young adults, these mothers shift their personal orientation away from children—and the nurturing outlook that prevails when children are young—and back to self and spousal relations as their more competitive and assertive selves predominate (Bedford, 1989a). The broad context for this shift was discussed in Chapter 3; here, we simply want to underscore the point that this shift also means they may become less tolerant of failings they perceive in the behavior of their siblings. It appears these middle-aged siblings "either do not know how they feel about their siblings or they are only aware of one valence of their feelings, positive or negative" (Bedford, 1989a, p. 221). (While this may indeed be the case, it could also be true that these respondents are just not very good at communicating how they feel about their sisters and brothers.)

Communication problems and life cycle changes can make siblings quite vulnerable to the strains involved in sharing parental caregiving. In a recent study of 141 sibling pairs, middle-aged caregivers were found to be egocentrically biased in their perceptions of sibling contributions. Respondents "reliably overestimated their contributions to their parents' welfare, felt the situation would be more fair if their siblings contributed more, and expected their siblings to disagree with them" (Lerner, Somers, Reid, Chiriboga, & Tierney, 1991, p. 754). In another report coming from the same study, the researchers (Lerner et al., 1988) suggested that perceptions of inequitable relative contributions to caregiving often are not resolved. The result is that previously existing identity-level relationships, those expressing a great deal of psychological closeness, are not always reestablished.

As we argued in the introduction to this chapter, however, attachment relations between siblings often are able to reassert themselves in later life because the obstacles to their expression (e.g., caring for their children) have been removed or at least minimized. In research that explored later-life sibling relations with 30 men and 30 women, subjects said the most important reason for their increased contact with siblings was that, because they had reached the life cycle stage in which they were no longer working or involved in active parenting, they had the time necessary for more frequent interactions (Gold, 1987). These siblings also reported that as they grew older they were able to forgive and forget old hurts, found themselves worrying more about the physical and financial health of their siblings, and felt a greater sense of filial responsibility. Bedford's (1992) recent work on the "least favored sibling" confirms this development. In mid-life, with parents still living, least-favored siblings may blame their brothers and sisters for parental favoritism. After parents have died, least-favored status no longer creates the same impediment to good sibling relations.

As the population in general ages, these reunions or resurgences in sibling attachment are being reported more often in the popular press. A recent story in a local newspaper on the closeness of sisters cited the work of Gold and quoted the famous sister pair of Abigail van Buren (Dear

Abby) and Ann Landers. Landers remarked, "We did have problems at one time. It's all gone and forgotten . . . . When we're together, we talk all night" (Krier, 1992). Abby and Ann are atypical in that they are identical twins who were not apart for one day until, in a double wedding, they were married. At the same time, now in their 70s, they are typical of sisters getting over sibling rivalries once they are beyond active child rearing and caregiving for parents.

A majority of the respondents in Gold's (1987) research said that their feelings toward their brothers and sisters had changed as they grew older. They expressed a need to be psychologically close. The responses given by these siblings suggest some possible sources of this need: an awareness that they were getting closer to the end of their lives, widowhood, a sense of task specificity (Connidis & Davies, 1990), and a strong tie to their family of origin (Pulakos, 1990). In a study by Martin Matthews (1992), one widow expressed it this way:

In my opinion I had the best mother, father, brother, and sisters that ever lived. I get a lot of comfort from that fact. We were very close.

Gold's (1987) respondents had an enhanced sense of the importance of siblings, simply because they existed and had a shared personal history. This shared history was a special connection for one widow in the Martin Matthews study (1992):

I think you should keep in touch with family. It's kinda nice. I enjoy talking with my sister. We can talk about people and experiences in the past that I can't talk about with anyone else.

In this sense then, the primary support siblings provided to these respondents was emotional in nature. Some invoke the support even after their siblings have died.

Because sisters typically experience more contact with siblings than do brothers and because usually they enjoy close relations, siblings can make a considerable contribution to a widow's well-being (O'Bryant, 1988). One widow's comment explains both her affection and a reason for making contact:

I have to keep in touch with her all the time. It's the love you have for them. I have to find out if she is all right.   **(Martin Matthews, 1992)**

The difference that often occurs between a sister's feelings about her brothers and her feelings about her sisters is reflected by a widow who said

I have never disowned my brother. We had a few hard feelings between us and finally I went my way and he went his. We still get together once in awhile. I tried to help him all I could. I was very close to my oldest sister Anne. We shared our problems and helped one another. My sisters and I helped each other and visited together and so on.   (Martin Matthews, 1992)

This kind of support provides psychological security: Someone who knows, understands, and cares for you is out there. If an instrumental need arises or a confidant is desired, then that person can be contacted. Revocable detachment (Connidis, 1991) is one way to think of this process. The detachment is revoked when a dormant attachment relationship with a sibling is made active. A person may activate the attachment by simply finding comfort in thinking of a sibling, by reaching out to confide in a sibling, or by enjoying the company of a sibling.

Sex Differences in Support from Sibs

Earlier we noted that older people more often consider their siblings to be confidants than to be companions (Connidis & Davies, 1990). Does this suggest that they are also friends? In a study that surveyed 300 respondents who had a sibling, it was found that while sister–sister dyads have more contact than other sibling dyads, members of these dyads are no more likely to declare each other a friend than to declare a brother a friend (Connidis, 1989c). The point, we think, is that attachment does not require contact, and so contact in itself does not predict friendship. To underscore this, the findings of this study also revealed that not declaring the high-contact sibling a friend did not mean a lack of emotional closeness.

So much of the research on siblings has shown that sister–sister dyads have more contact and attachment relations with each other than did any dyad involving brothers that brothers have been almost ignored. However, the findings of one of the very few studies involving brothers would be worth pursuing in future research. The respondents in this study were 49 brother dyads, mean age 51, who did not have a sister (Matthews, Delaney, & Adamek, 1989). The outcome variable, level of affiliation, allowed sibling relations to be organized into four levels: disparate, disaffiliated, lukewarm, and closely affiliated (p. 63). The findings, tentative at best, suggested that geographic and age proximity were important to level of affiliation. Marital status was also relevant; respondents who were single or remarried were more likely to be classified as disaffiliated or disparate. Taken as a whole, the results of this study indicate that brothers warrant more attention; they appear to have ongoing sibling relationships that, while less likely to be affectionate and close than those of sisters, are an important part of their support networks.

Conclusions and Summary

In this chapter we have tied the relationships among siblings to the long-term reciprocity and attachment that have been our theoretical ground points throughout. Attachment theory explains the affectionate closeness and psychological security that siblings provide for each other without necessitating face-to-face contact. In fact, siblings do contact each other, and sisters do so more frequently than any other dyad, because they want to see a confidant, share personal histories, check on their sibling's well-being, and contribute to their own.

For a couple growing older, no longer involved in active parenting, siblings are likely to be important sources of support. Caregiving responsibilities, and sometimes old hurts, can strain these affectionate relations, but generally ties to the family of origin and lifelong reciprocity overcome such strains and enable mutual support.

Having said this, while the research literature has expanded by leaps and bounds over the past five years, there is still much we do not know. Very little is known of differences in sibling relations due to ethnicity, family structure, or even time. Existing "longitudinal" studies typically include only two data points separated by no more than a few years. It is likely that the attachment we have found to characterize sibling relations for white, middle-class couples with children will be typical of sibling relations in other contexts, but the expression of this attachment will vary with the circumstances. As one widow remarked,

I am friends with both my sisters. My younger sister was adopted out at birth when my mother died. She did not find out she was adopted until after she was married. Since then the two of us have been thick as flies.

                                                            (Martin Matthews, 1992)

 **Among Friends and Family**

The Tindale and Norris families are friends. Their children play and attend school together. The couples converse casually in person and by telephone, and occasionally meet for an "adults only" evening. Joseph and Joan work together, and their spouses, Helen and Randy, have participated in the same community activities. Both families have met for birthday parties, informal dinners, and impromptu visits.

Many writers have commented that friendship, such as that shared by our two families, is sustained by the pleasure that all of us derive from each other's company. This enjoyment leads us to seek each other out because we want to, rather than because we feel obliged to, as family members often do. This has led one researcher to comment that it is nothing short of a miracle that friendships survive (Wiseman, 1986). They appear fragile, and uncontrolled by formal institutions, yet they are remarkably stable.

Obviously, it is important for friends to enjoy one another. Nevertheless, if enjoyment were the only the reason for a friendship, it would, indeed, be fragile. Beneath the fun, there are far more significant purposes to friendship: to provide advice, moral support, and tangible aid. Adults rely on their friends for help in dealing with concerns of day-to-day life and in coping with major life crises. In fact, friends may call upon each other more often than upon family members to provide both tangible and intangible support. This strengthens a friendship and gives it a central role. Again, consider the authors' families: Neither has grandparents who reside nearby and can provide assistance without notice. Thus, in emergencies we rely upon one another. When the youngest of the Norris children fell down the stairs, for example, this required a fast trip to the hospital, and someone to look after the other two children. Because Randy Norris was at work in another city, Helen Tindale dropped everything and came to the rescue. The following week, the Tindale's baby-sitter became ill on a night both parents had meetings to attend. Joan Norris cared for their children. In both circumstances, the support provided was part of an ongoing relationship characterized by reciprocity.

What Friends Are For

Like the authors' families, most people "get by with a little help from [their] friends." Why are friends such an important source of help? There are two general answers to this question (Norris & Rubin, 1984). First, friends bolster us emotionally, providing affection and a sense of belonging. Such extrafamilial attachments are critical to good mental health whether we are preschoolers or centenarians. Second, friends promote and maintain good psychological functioning by encouraging us to compare our view of the world to theirs. We are prompted to look beyond the norms and rules of our families to understand other perspectives. Such challenges permit us to confirm our perceptions, or to refine or alter them.

There is extensive research on these processes in the friendships of children (see Norris & Rubin, 1984, for a review). Adolescents, for example, rely on friends to help them separate from their families and understand the new social environment that they are entering, and to supply a peer group with whom they can feel a sense of belonging. This group may provide a means of bridging the values and beliefs of their parents' generation with those of younger adults. This may be particularly important when adolescents are members of a minority whose older members are not likely to share the views of the dominant culture. A study of Mormon teenagers, for example, found that peers supported one another's choice of dating partners in accordance with the rule of endogamy, marrying within their own group, set down by their religion (Markstrom-Adams, 1991). This strategy probably minimized intergenerational conflict while promoting a sense of peer group membership.

The available information on friendship during the adult years suggests that friends continue to provide supports throughout the life span. Research on social support in times of stress provides a good illustration of how this might work (e.g., Gottlieb, 1983). Often a person will have experience with the same problem that a friend is facing. This experienced person may be able to use his or her store of knowledge and coping strategies to help reduce the friend's anxiety, to provide supportive feedback that may short-circuit the friend's possible feelings of self-recrimination, and to bolster the friend's self-esteem and feelings of personal control. The person may also provide problem-solving strategies and tangible aid. Because of similar circumstances and values, friends may become at least as important a resource as members of the extended family who have shared much less.

Studies of support during widowhood illustrate this process quite well. Older married women are likely to become widows in later life because of differences in longevity between men and women. When a woman loses her spouse, she is likely to find support from another widow within her circle of friends. This friend can help her cope with her grief and provide practical tips on arranging the funeral and managing her finances. Research has shown that this help from friends is more important to widows' adjustment in the long run than the support of their children (Vachon & Stylianos, 1988).

There is a substantial literature on friendship in adulthood. Unfortunately, much of this work does not discuss friendship within the context of family relationships. This has made it difficult to determine the relative importance of friendships and family relationships. The purpose of this chapter is to explore friendship through the family life cycle from the perspective of the marital couple in an intergenerational family, and to raise these questions: What kind of transactions occur between friendships and intergenerational family relationships as adults grow older? What kinds of aid and support are exchanged by friends, and are these supports different from those provided by family members? How is this assistance negotiated and understood by everyone involved? In answering these questions, we will consider the couple at three different points in the intergenerational family life cycle: the early years, the parental years, and the postparental period.

It is clearly important to discuss the influence of variations in family structure and ethnicity on friendship. One researcher has commented that we should doubt the validity of any model for studying friendship that overlooks the cultural or historical context (Hess, 1989). Nevertheless, there is very little information that would permit anything more than just doubt at this point. The available literature allows some consideration of the effect on friendship of changing family forms such as the increase in single parent families. Potential ethnic differences in friendship, on the other hand, generally have been ignored (Blieszner, 1989). Thus, the questions posed in this chapter can be answered only partially until we know more about cultural subgroups in our society (Hess, 1989).

A Look at Couples and Their Friends Across the Life Span

Early Marriage: Couples and Singles

"You may be doing something unforgivable in the eyes of your single friends: Getting married," suggests an article in a newspaper supplement for brides ("Getting Married," 1990). The author notes that a bride's single friends may be jealous or even hostile at the thought of her marriage, and because of this, "friendshifts" are almost inevitable.

Marriage *does* take a toll on friendship. When people marry, their old friendships must coexist with a significant new relationship (Berger & Kellner, 1970). This coexistence does not, however, imply equality. Men and women still marry with the thought that their relationship must be the primary bond in their lives (Lamanna & Reidmann, 1988). Thus, friends can be regarded as "trespassers" who may cause trouble if they intrude into the marital relationship (McDonald & Osmond, 1980). To avoid causing jealousy in their partners, then, spouses may decide to discard a friend rather than reworking the relationship with him or her to make it less competitive:

She trashed our friendship. You'd think I never existed. I didn't ask her to choose between me and him. I never wanted *all*, but she didn't have to give me *nothing* either.

   (a man speaking about a former friend; Pogrebin, 1987, pp. 67–68)

Why do married couples feel that such drastic action is necessary? Between them and their single friends there are three potential sources of problems that may lead to the termination of the friendships. The first of these "flashpoints" (Pogrebin, 1987) arises from a decline in personal resources that can be expended on friendship after an individual marries. Emotional and physical energy, time, and sometimes money are now likely to be restricted for both husband and wife. Whatever is available is used first to maintain the marriage. If a friend has come to expect that certain kinds of help will be extended or received and this is now less likely, the relationship may be on shaky ground. Nevertheless, it should also be recognized that dual-income couples whose members share interests and friends may actually have more personal resources than before the marriage to devote to friendships. Clearly, the nature of the marital relationship must be considered when predicting the nature of interactions with friends.

A friend's expectations that support from a married friend will remain at the same level as before the marriage may put wives in a particularly difficult situation. This is because their friendships are based on ideals of nurturance and reciprocity (Wright, 1989), qualities they also are expected to show in interactions with their husbands. Thus a woman's friendships and marital relationship may end up in direct conflict, with the result that only those relationships that do not threaten the marriage may be maintained (Fischer & Oliker, 1983). Men, on the other hand, have a different experience because their same-sex friendships are based on activity and common interests (Wright, 1989). There is thus little direct competition for emotional support and disclosure. These can be provided in the spousal relationship. Men may not have time for all of their single friends, but it does not appear as painful to them as it does to women to discard some of them or to see them less often.

A second problem in the relationships between couples and their single friends is the diminished number of shared experiences. Single friends are still likely to be part of the world of dating and courtship, a world that requires more varied and energetic social activity. The couple, on the other hand, is likely to be less socially active or to restrict their engagements to other married friends. When they include a single person in any of these events, they may also invite someone of the opposite sex, an act that unmarried friends find irritating and sometimes insulting.

"It's like Noah's ark in my neighborhood. If you're not a couple, you can't come aboard" (Pogrebin, 1987).

A diminished number of shared experiences among newly coupled individuals and their single friends can contribute to the third problem area, differing perceptions of each other and of the friendship. There is a tendency in our marriage-oriented society, and in the scholarly research on families, to assume that one must eventually marry to meet intimacy needs (Norris, 1990). Couples then may begin to view themselves as successful and their single friends as suffering from a case of arrested development. The singles may reciprocate with the belief that marrieds are stuffy and uninteresting. Such divergent attitudes and defensive posturing can come between married people and their single friends.

The difficulties encountered in making the transition from "single" to "couple" may have costs for friendship but rewards for intergenerational family relationships. The older couple whose comments began Chapter 4 noted with some irony that grown children tend to disappear into their peer relationships until they marry and begin families of their own. Then "it's 'hey, Mom, hey Dad, have you got this, can I have some of that?'" (61-year-old grandfather, Norris & Tari, 1985). These requests for help and newly shared interests in family life seem to reinforce intergenerational bonds of attachment. Where there was conflict over the children's choice of friends during their adolescent years, parents may feel a great sense of relief. One 65-year-old father's comments reflect his efforts at remaining philosophical about the trials of adolescence, but very happy when his daughter rejoined the fold:

With teenage kids, there is always a gap, I think, in all families because they have different ideas of what should be, different moral standards and it is hard for parents to understand. This is part of growing up and so you have to join the ranks or you have problems. It was hard to resolve differences with my daughter. She left the house for a while and lived with someone which was outside of our faith; we are Jewish. Gradually you begin to accept things and then she left the boy and married a nice Jewish boy and everything turned out okay.   **(Norris & Tari, 1985)**

In some families, however, children may keep the friends and lifestyles acquired as they were growing up, perhaps marrying a member of their peer group not sanctioned by their parents. Such a marriage could isolate the young couple from both their single friends and their extended families. In the case below, a 62-year-old mother interprets her alienation from her daughter as a consequence of her son-in-law's jealousy. An equally plausible explanation is the reluctance of this adult daughter to re-establish a conflictual relationship:

> **I was too strict with my children . . . . Even when they were twenty-one, they had to be in by midnight no matter what. I was too strict. [Now I am] far apart from my daughter out West. Now I don't mean far apart in distance—I don't see her because of her husband. That's one thing I would like to see changed. Nothing has ever happened but I think it is just jealousy on his part—jealous of her being so close to us.**   (Norris & Tari, 1985)

Who Will Be Our Friends? Developing a New Network

Newlyweds need to reinforce their interdependence with each other and also with extended family, especially if the couple's marriage did not receive family approval. In this way, they move from feeling like "married singles" with different lives and aspirations to interacting as family members. Their goal is to evolve a warm, highly supportive identity relationship (Lerner, 1981). The development of new friendships, shared by both spouses, is an important means to this end. In particular, such couples attempt to build friendships with other people in the same situation: newlyweds (Titus, 1980).

Finding compatible "couple" friends is not always easy (Lasswell & Lasswell, 1991). There are a number of informal rules that appear to guide the development and maintenance of such relationships. First, the wife typically selects an eligible couple. An important criterion here is that she is already close, or at least friendly, with the woman in the other couple. Second, the husbands must like one another. They may even have been friends as singles before their marriages. Third, the wives and husbands must be willing to accept each other's spouse, but not to like them too much!

Once all of these requirements are met, the couples can become a significant resource for one another, providing aid and advice on a day-to-day basis. This interaction and support helps each couple avoid a major pitfall common in young marriages: isolation from other relationships (Fine, 1991). Under the best circumstances, the same-sex spouses become close individual friends and confidants. The cross-sex pairs may also become friends, but, as we will see, this situation is fraught with potential trouble.

The Cross-Gender Complication

Before they are married, almost all men and a majority of women can name a person of the opposite sex as one of their close friends. Only two-thirds of newly married men and about half of newly married women, on the other hand, report such a relationship (Rose, 1985). Part of the reason for this change may be an artifact of the research: Before they are married, individuals name their potential mate as a "friend"; after marriage, they do not because this person now has a more important status. Nevertheless, this does not appear to be the whole story. There are important social conventions governing cross-gender friendships that lead to their reduction or termination after marriage. These norms seem to be different for men and women.

Single men often view their cross-gender friendships as potential romantic attachments (Wright & Bergloff, 1984). Even when a man is "just friends" with a woman, he values this relationship precisely because it is with a woman: It provides support and allows self-disclosure not common in his same-sex relationships. If after marriage he has fewer female friends, it may be because these needs are now fulfilled by his relationship with his spouse.

"Women's friendships with men are relatively unimportant" (Wright, 1989, p. 206). This unequivocal conclusion is supported by many studies indicating that women turn to other women to fulfill needs for interpersonal intimacy and support (e.g., Rubin, 1985). Their cross-gender friendships are likely to provide support, for example, tangible household repairs, rather than emotional support and are therefore less significant than their same-sex relationships. Perhaps this is one reason why women report having fewer male than female friends, especially after marriage. Another reason, of course, is to avoid problems in their marriage: Remember the woman who "trashed" her relationship with a male friend?

Because even a married man may see cross-gender friendships as warm, supportive, and incipiently sexual (Pogrebin, 1987), he may have difficulty understanding his wife's perspective. Ann Landers's reply to a puzzled wife reflects this problem. Landers clearly feels that a spouse is entitled to some say in how his partner manages a close cross-sex relationship. This view is quite consistent with current social norms:

Dear Ann Landers: I have been happily married for 21 years. I love my husband dearly, but for the first time in our marriage we have an issue which we cannot resolve. I recently took a class and became friendly with a single man, age 35. (I'm 44.) After the class was over, we wanted to continue the friendship, so occasionally we meet for lunch or a movie when I am in his area on business. He lives 70 miles away. He tells me about his dates, and we catch up on what's new in each other's lives. Then we go our separate ways.

I naturally told my husband about this. It is just a friendship, no sex. My husband has not spoken to me for three days because I saw this man last week . . . . Can't a man and woman be platonic friends anymore?

FROZEN OUT IN MAINE

Dear Frozen: Obviously your husband feels threatened by this man. There is something about the relationship that bothers him. If your marriage is important to you, you ought to give some thought to a compromise.

How about double-dating with the man and one of the women he is taking out? Surely the four of you could have a pleasant time together and your husband would have no cause to be suspicious. I recommend it.

("Ann Landers," 1991)

Perhaps the treacherous waters of cross-sex friendship can be navigated more easily when such friends are also intergenerational relatives. In one recent survey, 85% of young adults listed relatives as among their closest friends (Norris, 1992). Many of these friends (25%) were much older. Comparable responses have also come from older adults: When cross-gender friendships are reported, they are likely to involve relatives (siblings, nieces and nephews, cousins, and in-laws (Norris & Rubin, 1988), who may also be considerably younger (Knudsen, 1988). This cross-gender friendship described by Knudsen (1988), for example, is unlikely to cause either spouse anxiety:

Mrs. Patterson is a 72-year-old married woman who reported that her son-in-law is a cross-sex friend. They have known each other for about 15 years. They visit on the phone and in person about once a week. Contact initiation is mixed and when they get together it is to share a meal with Mrs. Patterson's husband, their daughter, and the grandchildren. During these get-togethers they visit, watch television and play with the grandchildren. Mrs.

Patterson feels "very close" to her son-in-law and doesn't feel that their relationship has changed over the years.   **(p. 100)**

Working It Out: Reformulating and Rethinking Friendships
Developing and maintaining a friendship is hard work. As we have seen, finding a place for friendships within the newly formed marital relationship, and in an intergenerational context, can be complicated and stressful. Nevertheless, the rewards are clearly worthwhile: pleasure, support, and guidance. How then can a couple build successful friendships once the friends have been selected?

Good communication is essential when husbands and wives are negotiating their way through friendships. There must be discussion of the rules for relationships outside the family that each spouse learned from his or her family of origin. For example, How much help can be expected from friends? Of what type? Under what circumstances? Is immediate reciprocity required when assistance is given? Do the needs of extended family members supersede those of friends? Although there is evidence that friendships are governed by some common rules, especially relating to exchange (Argyle & Henderson, 1984), these rules may have more or less salience depending on the individual's gender, ethnicity, family background, and friendship history. Couples must clarify and negotiate approaches to friendship that meet the needs of their new family situation.

The Child-Rearing Years: Friendship's Best and Worst of Times

Most young married couples eventually have children, and many have them within two years of marriage (Nett, 1988). Thus, old friendships which survived the marriage of singles, as well as new "couple" friendships, must weather another change: children. Problems of scarce resources, diminished numbers of shared experiences, and conflicting perceptions once again may cause conflict within friendships. Single, childless friends may now feel even more like "trespassers" or even "thieves," robbing married friends of time they might spend with spouse and children (Rubin, 1985). Coupled, but childless, friends who once shared so much with the new parents may feel similarly dispossessed and shut out of the relationship. For some friendships, the strain may be too much and the relationship may be terminated (Brenton, 1974).

Friendships with other parents, however, may show just the opposite pattern of development: Sharing the intense moments of childbearing and child-rearing can make couples even more interconnected and interdependent. Friends can provide advice on parenting and tangible assistance with children. They can also act as "rescuers," intervening when a parent's situation becomes too stressful. Consider this example: A woman noticed that her friend, a working wife and mother, needed to take a break from her responsibilities. The mother tells it this way, clearly appreciative of her friend's intervention, though rueful that she needed it:

I had come home from a business trip on an earlier flight than I'd planned [and my daughter was still at school]. The mother of one of [my daughter's] friends happened to see my car in the driveway. She came in and dragged me out for an ice cream cone. Now this seems goddamned stupid, but I hadn't done anything like that in a year. I just left my house spontaneously, knowing that I had a million things to do because I'm never home to do them. We walked to the ice cream store, chatting all the way. Then we came back to my house and had a couple of glasses of wine while the kids played. I never do that. *Never.* (Kinsella, 1986, p. 189)

If parenthood makes friendship intense and crisis oriented, how do such relationships survive? After all, friends are not bound to each other by duty or formal roles, as are family members, and so are not required to cope with each other's disasters and day-to-day hassles. One of the answers to this question appears to be the flexible approach to equity and reciprocity taken by friends during this period. Research suggests that friendships are most successful when help is reciprocated (Ingersoll-Dayton & Antonucci, 1988). Yet anecdotal accounts, including the ones which introduced this chapter, indicate that reciprocation is interpreted very loosely among friends. Why is this the case?

The probable answer lies in the attachment that friends have for one another during this time in the family life cycle, and the implication of this attachment for their expectations about equitable support. As we have seen, shared experiences and perceptions cement a relationship and move it from the realm of specific exchanges to something more communal (Mills & Clark, 1982). With time, there develops a sense of global reciprocity in which there is little or no expectation of immediate repayment for support provided (Wentowski, 1981). Friends are then described as being "just like family" or, as some researchers have termed them, "fictive kin" (Schusky, 1965; Mac Rae, 1992).

Mothers' and Fathers' Friendships

Many authors have noted the importance that female friends have for women during the years when children are young. These friendships may be especially important now because new grandmothers are more likely to be in the paid labor force than ever before (Matras, 1990) and unable to provide much support for their daughters. Mothers, then, can provide one another with counsel, child care relief, and outgrown clothes! Stay-at-home mothers can also provide a reference group for one another, as is reflected in the words of this mother of three children who feels like "an endangered species" (Scharrenbroich, 1986). She related that her neighborhood friends were essential to her well-being when the children were babies:

On rainy days we would visit each other for coffee. We could spend a whole morning in somebody's kitchen while the kids played in the next room. We all had backyards and we'd sit outside and drink iced coffee in the summer and let the kids play in a wading pool or with the hose. We'd just talk, trade recipes, joke, just talk. At that time nobody thought about a meaningful life, or that this was not important. Many of us felt tedium, which is why it was so good to have each other . . . . I was never lonely. There was tremendous support, and a lot of shared babysitting.   **(Scharrenbroich, 1986, p. 147)**

The shared experiences of mothers, and the friendship of their children, further reinforce the relationship between couples. Again at the instigation of the wives, social events are planned for these couples, and often the children as well. The men appear to go along for the ride, accepting the friendship of the couples their wives have chosen, and perhaps involving themselves in shared activities with the other husbands. At this period in their lives, men seem less likely to develop their own special, individual friendships. In fact, men report, having fewer same-sex friends and seeing the friends they do have less frequently (Reisman, 1981). It has been suggested that men are too immersed in career development to put the effort into friendship (Reisman, 1981), but recent evidence suggests that working men and women are equally involved in their jobs (Hatch & Bulcroft, 1992). Perhaps another explanation is likely: As is true throughout marriage, men rely almost exclusively on their spouses for the fulfillment of intimacy needs; women do not (Wright, 1989).

Changes in Family Composition

The carefully constructed friendships among coupled parents can face severe challenges when families experience separation or divorce. Good friends are necessary to help negotiate and adapt to marital break-up (Pogrebin, 1987). Nevertheless, good friends may not be able to cope with the experience themselves, nor provide the support and assistance that newly single parents need (Bohannon, 1970). Reconstructing a friendship between couples may be extremely difficult, especially when the intact couple must weigh its relative attachments to each ex-spouse. What seems to happen, then, is that the wife is maintained as a friend because she was close to the woman, or the husband is kept as a friend because he seems so needy, but there may be no room for both (Pogrebin, 1987).

Divorce can also disrupt intergenerational in-law relationships that have evolved into friendships. The available research on cross-sex friendships discussed earlier in this chapter suggests that many such relationships involve people related to the couple by marriage (Knudsen, 1988; Norris & Rubin, 1988). These friendships may be very difficult to maintain at a time when older parents feel they must support their adult children. Contact between parents and their adult child tends to increase after separation and divorce, but strain and open conflict are likely to prevent increased interaction with children-in-law (Gladstone, 1989).

Despite strain and problems with divided loyalty, however, it still seems likely that a close friendship between a mother-in-law and daughter-in-law, for example, could weather a divorce. This becomes even more likely if the daughter-in-law has custody of the grandchildren. Research has shown that grandparents want to maintain contact with grandchildren, and that a history of positive interaction with the child-in-law predicts that this will actually happen (Gladstone, 1988; 1989). Visits with grandchildren, then, probably legitimize and facilitate the continuing friendship between parent and child-in-law.

Working It Out: Nurturing Multiple Relationships

During one of Joan's graduate courses on social relationships, she asks students to talk about their friendships: What does it mean to be a "good" friend? Typically, each student feels that good friends give each other their time and energy. The single, childless graduate students feel that they have little time and energy, and express some regret that they are not doing what they once did for their friends. But they still see their friends and are relatively content with the situation. Married students with children are almost unable to answer the question, except with other questions: How can I even *see* my friends with the other commitments that I have? How can I make my friends understand my lifestyle? How can I make them wait for me until I have more time to spend with them? Even if they do wait, will I still enjoy their company? For these students, like many other parents struggling with multiple roles, the issue of maintaining friendships arouses feelings of anxiety and guilt.

Rather than becoming paralyzed by such feelings, couples must accept the situation, and make some decisions about how they will manage their friendships at this point in the family life cycle. Once again, negotiation and problem-solving skills become important.

If the family does not have the resources to maintain all friendships, how should the available resources be allocated? Couples are likely to adopt a policy of distributive justice based on maintaining long-term attachments as well as short-term exchange relationships. The most time, effort, affection, and tangible support will be invested in people, probably family members and close friends, with whom couples share an identity relationship: These friendships are likely to withstand the test of time and life events. They are also likely, according to one researcher, to be those relationships shared with others of the same ethnic and religious background (Litwak, 1989).

The remaining resources will be put toward those more transient, probably unitlike relationships that are clearly linked to specific events and family life cycle stage. These friendships are often the product of sharing the experience of parenting young children, and are characterized by immediate reciprocity. Couples have such friendships with neighbors, other bench-warming parents of the Little League, co-workers, and members of their prenatal class.

Making conscious choices about which friendships to maintain and how much to invest in them is difficult, but such a strategy helps busy parents to cope with multiple roles and demands. Clarifying the current "rules of friendship" helps avoid conflict and overcommitment. The anxiety and guilt of our married students might be lessened if they were to "edit" their friendships, developing and maintaining those with people they are deeply attached to, and realizing that others will come and go depending on changing circumstances.

The Postparental Years

**Well if you don't enjoy [your friends], then your life becomes very narrow
and self-centered, I think. And their lives, their joys, their problems: we
share with them. I think it helps and it is good for us and makes us appreciate
our blessings more. And you can progress more if you are sharing ideas with
others.   (a 70-year-old wife; Norris & Tari, 1985)**

Once couples have launched their children (or at least raised them to
adulthood, even if they won't leave home!), they are freer to devote their
energies to nonfamily relationships. It is not surprising, then, that research has noted the importance of friendship to people no longer involved in active parenting (Adams & Blieszner, 1989). In particular,
long-term friendships have special significance for many people; they
often are based on shared ethnic or religious group membership, and on a
wealth of shared experience and affection (Litwak, 1989). As the woman
quoted above notes, old friends can supply deep emotional fulfillment and
promote good psychological functioning. In fact, there is some evidence
that people are most happy with friends who show evidence of successful
aging and strive to promote it in others (Fisher, Reid, & Melendez, 1989).

This strong attachment to old friends can be both a blessing and a
problem for postparental couples. Clearly, old friends can fulfill important supportive functions, but they may also interfere with the development of new relationships at a time when social losses are common. In
later life, people become increasingly selective about their friends, pre-
ferring those with whom the "payoff"—positive interactions and affect—
is more certain (Fredrickson & Carstensen, 1990). This preference may
result in couples avoiding opportunities for new relationships, thus re-
stricting the network of people who could provide them with support.

One researcher, Matthews (1986), has suggested that enduring characteristics determine who will try to make new friends late in life. From
retrospective accounts of their friendships in adulthood, she divided a
sample of older people into two types: those who are highly selective, or
"discerning," making few friends who are not replaced if they are lost
through conflict or death; and those who are "independent," rarely making friends at all (Matthews, 1986). Nevertheless, these types are rare,
suggesting that other factors are more important in explaining the strong
preference for familiar faces.

One such factor may be the nature of the exchange relationship with friends as it occurs in later life. As we have noted, important relationships are characterized by a norm of global reciprocity: help may not be reciprocated immediately, or may never be returned. Having only close friends appeals to older couples who prefer not to be beholden to strangers whom they may be unable to repay (Jones & Vaughn, 1990; Wentowski, 1981). When asked to give help to or receive help from anyone other than close friends or family members, older adults make it clear that they operate under strict rules of immediate reciprocity (Ingersoll-Dayton & Antonucci, 1988). Inequities, particularly when the older person is overbenefited, can lead to lower self-esteem and feelings of dependency and depression (Roberto & Scott, 1986; Rook, 1987). Thus, when a husband and wife lack the close friends with whom they can interact under conditions of global reciprocity, they prefer to rely on one another instead. This can maintain a strong marital relationship, but it also can lead to the isolation of the couple from helpful informal supports (Day, 1985). In this 85-year-old husband's account of his current life, the only meaningful peer relationship that he reports is with his wife. It is clear that her loss would leave him isolated and lonely:

I don't associate too much with the men in our apartment building [even though] everyone is very nice and always says good morning or afternoon when I go down for the mail . . . but my wife and I can always hold a good conversation because we came from the same town and knew one another when we were young. We will soon be married 59 years.

I've been thinking a lot about old age. To some it is very hard going, but to others like ourselves it is sort of a comforting experience. Our families are grown; we aren't responsible for them any more. Of course, you worry over them and you worry over your life partner, but on the whole it is a satisfying time. (Norris, 1978)

Widowhood: Uncoupling the Friendship

Carefully maintained couple relationships can experience profound upheaval when one or more of the spouses die. The attachment that kept friends together may be weakened for many reasons, some of which are reminiscent of the problems couples had in establishing friendships when newly married. There are fewer shared experiences, including unshared bereavement, between a couple and a newly "single" person; there may be difficulties in maintaining the cross-gender tie in the relationship; it may be impossible to balance exchanges among unequal numbers of people (Allen & Adams, 1989). Whatever the reason, widowed people report decreasing numbers of interactions with their married friends as the length of their widowhood increases (Lopata, 1979). Instead, women may seek the company of their widowed peers (Petrowsky, 1976) and adult children; men may remarry (Cleveland & Gianturco, 1976; Gentry & Shulman, 1988).

Friends and Children

Monday: My feelings are great disappointment about my children—my son's telling me he had forwarded a cheque for me which I did not ask for, and this is two weeks ago, so he lied to me. So I am very sad, not receiving such.

Thursday: Today was great! Not only one girl friend visited me, but another that I had not seen for months; we three went for a walk and had lunch at Eaton's; they both counteracted my great depression about my son's grief that he has caused me.

(from the diary of Mrs. Rosansky, physically disabled 75-year-old widow; Norris, 1978)

The importance of friends to well-being and self-esteem is underscored in later life. In fact, much to the surprise of many adult children, friendships are more important to successful aging than parent–child relationships (Blau, 1981; Ontario Gerontology Association, 1986). Thus, older couples are likely to prefer "intimacy at a distance" with their children, while sharing activities and support with their friends (Connidis, 1989b). Under normal circumstances this arrangement works well for all concerned. Busy children are not asked to provide help to parents; as we have seen in Chapter 3, it is often the other way around! Instead, couples rely on comfortable exchanges with friends based on a norm of generalized reciprocity.

Critical situations such as debilitating illness or widowhood change this arrangement and introduce upheaval into relationships with both friends and children. When the amount of help needed becomes great, older people turn to their offspring first (Connidis, 1989b). They feel that it is inappropriate to ask for so much from friends; indeed, when friends offer help in circumstances such as the care of a spouse with Alzheimer's disease, it is not expected and has little impact on satisfaction and depression (Pagel, Erdly, & Becker, 1989). What *is* expected is that friends will continue to show evidence of their attachment and affection, and not upset the caregiver (Pagel, Erdly, & Becker, 1989).

Unbalanced exchanges with children cause less trouble for the older couple, who may feel that they are drawing, for the first time, on a lifetime support bank (Ingersoll-Dayton & Antonucci, 1988). Thus, being overbenefited by children has been linked to satisfaction with the parent–child relationship (Rook, 1987). An even larger literature, however, attests to the problems that adult offspring have in maintaining this new arrangement: Caregiver burden can become enormous (e.g., Brody, 1985). The comments, above, of a frail widow suggest the difficulties inherent in parent–child exchanges. Mrs. Rosansky feels that her son has not provided enough support, and she is especially hurt when promised help does not arrive. It is certainly possible that her son feels that he has been supportive, however, and this time is simply tardy or forgetful. Regardless of who is correct, the power of Mrs. Rosansky's friends to help her cope with a distressing situation can clearly be seen through her delight with their attention.

Working It Out: The Importance of Flexibility
Early in marriage, couples follow rules of exchange and reciprocity fairly carefully in their friendships until strong attachments form. Later, during the parenting years, these rules may become more flexible as the ability to provide immediate reciprocation becomes more difficult. In the post-parental period, however, there is a renewed concern with reciprocity in relationships. This is probably due to feelings of increased dependency that occur when couples feel they are receiving more than they give. Nevertheless, a rigid adherence to exchange principles restricts social relationships unnecessarily. The older couple should be prepared to allow some asymmetry in their peer relationships.

A special problem in negotiating supportive relationships in later life involves expectations for adult children. Clear communication between spouses and with offspring is critical. Adult children may not understand why their help is not required, or even rebuffed, at one point and then demanded at another. Confusion, hurt, and anger may result when the older couple is not clear and direct about their changing needs, feelings about friends, and expectations about the parent–child relationship.

Again, some flexibility is necessary on everyone's part as new roles and supportive functions are negotiated (Norris & Forbes, 1987).

Summary and Conclusion

Research on adult friendship has been expanding. Nevertheless, little attention has been paid to this relationship within the context of marriage and parent–child relationships throughout the family life cycle. In this chapter, we explored what is known about the friendships of married people from the time they become spouses, through the years of their active parenthood, and into later life. Three general questions were considered: How do couples manage their friendships in the context of their family relationships? What kinds of aid and support are exchanged with friends? How is this assistance negotiated and understood by everyone involved?

Answering these questions revealed that there are a number of problems to be dealt with by couples concerning their friendships, a number of tasks to be completed, and a process that facilitates the successful management of friendships within the context of the marital relationship. First, the problems: Newlyweds discover that they have fewer personal resources to expend on friendship than they did before they were married. Further, the parties to a friendship may have different perceptions and experiences of friendship that lead to conflicting expectations. Couples with dependent children encounter even more competing demands on their time and energy, and more potential for misunderstanding between themselves and friends without partners or children. Older couples may restrict their friendships in favor of those with whom they share experiences and affection. This may prohibit the growth of new supportive relationships.

These problem areas suggest a number of developmental tasks that must be completed by the couple to promote good relationships with friends. Young, childless couples must determine where friends fit into their lives, and what kind of friends these will be—"his," "hers," singles, or marrieds. Young parents must learn to manage many friends, and relationships, and make hard choices about the quality of their friendships as well as the frequency of interaction and exchange. Postparental couples, strongly bound to old friends and ideas of global reciprocity, must remember the value of novelty in friendships and take a flexible approach to equity in all of their relationships.

The developmental tasks of friendship can be facilitated by good communication between spouses, the same strategy that enhances problem-solving throughout marriage. Talking about the special difficulties in managing friendships at specific points in the family life cycle clarifies potential problems and suggests solutions. For example, early in marriage the rules regarding friendship derived from the spouses' respective family of origin can be presented, and strategies compatible with the new family developed. Later, harried parents can determine which relationships are a priority based on criteria that can be jointly determined, for example, friends to whom the couple is most attached or who meet particular, immediate needs. For older husbands and wives, discussion can revolve around balancing the familiar with the stimulating. In deciding whether to maintain only the old network of friends or to actively acquire new relationships, questions such as these may be asked: What would happen if the old friends were lost? How much imbalance in exchanges with our peers are we willing to tolerate? Even if clear solutions seldom emerge from these discussions, the potential for conflict between spouses, and with friends, is lessened as issues are clarified and misperception minimized.

If we think back to the anecdote that began this chapter, and the experience of friendship that emerges from the research literature as we have reviewed it, our questions about the nature and quality of couples' friendships can be answered. We conclude that across the family life cycle, friendships are important in sustaining a good marital relationship *if* they change in their meaning and function along with the couple. On the whole, husbands and wives are good at sorting out which relationships can be incorporated successfully into their marriage and their extended families, and which must receive less attention or be terminated. We have seen that under the best circumstances friendships can be at least as important as family relationships in promoting couples' physical and emotional well-being.

Ultimately, however, these conclusions must be tempered with the caution that they are based on largely homogeneous samples of white, middle-class adults. Some gerontologists have turned their attention to the social networks of other countries, but with North America's increasingly multicultural makeup, we are perhaps more urgently in need of a look at the subgroups within our own society (Blieszner, 1989; Hess, 1989). At this point, there are few answers to the questions posed by one well-known researcher on friendships:

What about the poor who are not homeless, or Mexican-Americans, or inner-city minority populations? Do American Jews have different friendship patterns than born-again Christians? If so, why?   (Hess, 1989, p. 9)

Considering the intergenerational family issues dealt with in this book, we would like to add a further question: Are there ethnic variations in friendship that interact with similar ethnic variations in family functioning and support?

7 Conclusion

INTERVIEWER: Would you say that you are a close family?

MR. RYAN: I don't know . . . I'm quite different [from] my wife. If she had her way—she's a real mother hen type, O.K.?—she would have [our children and grandchildren] around here every day, 24 hours a day. With friends and families . . . well, I like my privacy and I want to do my thing. I enjoy them, I guess, on my terms. I think they have their life to live and I don't want them to feel that they've got to come around and see me. So, it's a question of degree. When the chips are down, they don't mind calling me, although I've told them some things they didn't like to hear, but they've thanked me afterwards. "Well," I said, "that's what fathers are for." So it's been that kind of relationship. As you can sense, my wife looks at things quite differently than I do, which, of course, causes a problem. But that's what makes life interesting.

(62-year-old engineer, married 35 years; Norris, 1981)

Mr. Ryan's comments about his family life as he approaches retirement highlight the two central themes of this book: the attachment and reciprocal support experienced, in varying degrees, by members of a couple. Any long-term marriage has qualities that attest to the attachment and interdependency of each spouse, regardless of perceived marital satisfaction. Mr. and Mrs. Ryan clearly are different from one another in the way that each would like to handle important relationships. Perhaps these preferences are based on gender-role socialization; perhaps they are due to different personality traits or social skills. Whatever the cause, they have resulted in tension within the couple between Mrs. Ryan's desire for frequent, intimate contact with significant others and Mr. Ryan's wish for less frequent, more distant interaction.

Although it is impossible from the husband's comments to determine the level of satisfaction each spouse feels within the marriage, it does seem clear that the couple has been able to negotiate some agreement over the troublesome issue of family contact and family support. Their four children and two grandchildren do not live with them; in fact, only two children live in the same city. Mr. Ryan reports that they still feel free to ask him for help, even when they do not like his advice, and apparently do so by telephone—probably a medium that suits his rather cool interpersonal style. One suspects, and hopes, that Mrs. Ryan has similar freedom to interact with her children in less formal, more intimate fashion. There is some evidence for this from Mr. Ryan's report that when their son was in a recent car accident out west, "he phoned his mother"! Apparently emotional support from his mother, rather than advice from his father ("He's got a few things to learn"), was what he needed.

This Book in the Context of Other Work on Intergenerational Relations

In recent years, there have been many discussions and studies of the family in later life. Most of this work, however, has retained a focus on the individual older person. Typically, researchers have been interested in a person's attitude toward a particular family issue or role. The question might be asked, as we have seen from research discussed in Chapter 4, What is it like to be a grandparent? Not surprisingly, answers to this question focus on particular feelings ("fun") or behaviors ("We go fishing together"), and do not place the experience within the context of all of the significant relationships in that older person's life. Also, such research rarely considers the perceptions of other family members, even the spouse, about the same relationship. A grandfather is just that and no more; his more central role as husband is not discussed, nor are his wife's impressions solicited.

Research on marriage and the family has been limited as well, but in a different way. Often the differing perspectives of spouses—for example, on parenting responsibilities—are considered, but the research seems firmly focused on one stage in the family life cycle: the active parenting years. Thus, one does not get a sense of the history and future of current marital relations. Some of the research discussed in Chapter 2 suggests that children may not, in fact, be all that damaging to marital satisfaction. Instead, existing strains may lead to unhappiness both immediately after a baby's birth and well into the future of the marriage.

This book has provided a look at intergenerational relations that goes beyond a focus on the individual, isolated from others and suspended at one moment in the family life cycle. Instead, we have considered the perspective of both members of a couple as they negotiate their changing relationships with each other, and with family and friends, throughout their lives. The main question addressed has been how couples maintain and strengthen their marital relationship within the development of family intergenerational relationships. This question has been considered within two conceptual frameworks, attachment and reciprocity. We have argued that marriages function well when there is sustained attachment, and when there is sensitivity to long-term issues of fairness, equity, and reciprocity.

The Conceptual Frameworks

Attachment

Attachment theory was developed to explain the strong bond that mothers and infants normally establish with one another (e.g., Bowlby, 1969). Researchers in the field of child development view secure attachment as the product of an ongoing, well-functioning relationship between parent and child. These researchers have produced evidence to support a link between early, secure attachments and healthy peer and family relationships later in childhood (LaFreniere & Sroufe, 1985).

Recently, some life-span researchers have suggested that the concept of attachment has explanatory power in the study of adult relationships (Tesch, 1989). It is questionable how much direct impact the security of the bond between mother and infant has on their later relationship.

Nevertheless, it seems likely that early positive interactions between parents and offspring are likely to mature into warm and responsible filial relationships later in the family life cycle. The evidence presented in this book is certainly supportive of such maturation: We have seen that parents, for example, continue to provide support and affection for adult children, and sometimes grandchildren, at a time when all expected the nest to be empty. Conversely, the care given by adult children to frail older parents is well documented in the gerontological literature (e.g., Morris & Sherwood, 1984).

We have argued that attachment is a concept relevant to all relationships, across the life span, not just those between parents and children. It is likely that secure attachments early in life set the stage for successful peer interactions in adulthood (Norris & Rubin, 1984; Tesch, 1989). One of the most important of these is the marital relationship. Evidence suggests that adults continue to look for relationships that provide the four characteristics found in the attachments of childhood: the need for proximity in times of stress; comfort when together; unease or anxiety when the significant person is inaccessible; and a sense of permanence (Bowlby, 1973; Weiss, 1982). We would add that secure relationships in adulthood are characterized by the reciprocal sharing of meaning, emotion, and support (West & Reiffer, 1987).

Reciprocity

The sharing of resources within families typically has been considered within the context of exchange theory (e.g., Dowd, 1975). This perspective, however, is limited by its mechanistic assumption that individuals, when in interaction with others, are motivated to maximize social rewards and minimize costs. The context of the exchange, and the history of the relationship, may be ignored entirely. Within this framework, a parent who "refilled" her nest with a newly divorced adult child and her offspring would expect immediate restitution, perhaps in the form of household labor, to preserve good parent–child interactions.

The perspective on social exchange adopted in this book is one based on global reciprocity. This concept fits well within a life-span view of individual and family development because it considers the biological, social, psychological, and historical context of social support. Thus, the mother who considers sharing a household with her independent daughter will base her decision on many factors: for example, her own health and need for assistance with household chores; the degree to which cohabitation will affect her relationships with others; the balance of her need for independence and her need for intimacy; and the mutual support that she and her offspring have shared in the past. A recent newspaper article provides some insights into such decision making. Mrs. Tennant, the widowed mother of six children, was approached by her daughter, the single mother of her two-year-old granddaughter, to share a home. She reports:

I was reluctant to alter our comfortable relationship by an overdose of propinquity, but welcomed the sound of voices in the evenings and the idea that [my daughter] would have company when she desired.

We discussed ground rules . . . but I've never been very good at putting my foot down, which probably explains why I have six children.

I think the trick to surviving this multigenerational existence is to sever the cord once and for all. For instance, I am no longer the mom, and I don't answer to the name. I'm sharing the house with people I like, but we're not responsible for one another's behavior or habits.

Some day my ladies will move on and I'll have to relearn the art of solitary living, but that's OK. Life is an adventure. Besides there are five more children waiting in the wings. **(Tennant, 1992)**

Mrs. Tennant did express some initial reluctance to accept this new arrangement and acknowledges that she has had trouble setting limits in the past. Nevertheless, she has been able to construct the situation in a way that is workable for her, while also understanding that it is probably temporary, and she may be required to adjust, once again, to an empty nest.

Attachment, Reciprocity, and Entitlement

Interpretations of the fairness of intrafamilial situations rest upon both the attachment of family members and the degree of global reciprocity experienced across the family life cycle (Avioli, 1989). In this book, Lerner's (1981) ideas of entitlement have been used to help clarify this relationship. As we have seen from all of the research reviewed, when family members feel that they share similar interests, beliefs, and feelings, their support for one another will feel fair and equitable. Such identity relationships can be threatened, however, when the demands for help become continual and excessive. If, for example, Mrs. Tennant's daughter asked for other kinds of support that were not agreed upon prior to their cohabitation, the growing imbalance in support might be harder to overlook. In Lerner's terms, the relationship might become one of unity, or even nonunity, rather than identity. As long as individuals are able to communicate and negotiate, however, this occurrence is not likely. Mrs. Tennant at first took a hard line on child care: "I . . . will baby-sit when hell freezes over." She amended this, however, to offer emergency care only: "We did agree that, in case of illness, I would bend the rules and babysit." Clearly this change was a result of continuing negotiation with her daughter.

What Was Covered

This book grew from our observation that parents and their grown children frequently find themselves in situations requiring mutual support and understanding. An older couple would like help when opening and closing the family cottage each year; their son needs a loan to make a down payment on a house; another son moves back home for six months when he is laid off; a daughter moves back in with her two children for eighteen months following a separation from her husband. From our own experience, our research, and that of others, it seemed that while such help is usually exchanged successfully, it still may cause concern, worry, or even conflict. Parents may ask themselves whether they are undermining the autonomy of their adult children by providing loans, gifts, or free co-residency; children may feel uncomfortable having a loan from their parents because they do feel their autonomy is compromised. As we have seen, sustained attachment between husband and wife and between parents and their children promotes feelings of fairness, but the successful resolution of any problem is not inevitable; it requires work.

Early in the marital relationship, couples work to emerge from a period of "attaching," wherein the relationship may still be tentative, to one of long-term secure attachment. Research discussed in Chapter 2 supports the view that individual needs merge with couple needs, and the basis for global, rather than specific and immediate, reciprocity is established. These feelings are intensified with the arrival of children, who make even more remote the possibility that one spouse can fulfill all the needs of the other, and do so immediately. During these busy years, successfully married young couples appear to make ongoing efforts to talk to one another and to clarify feelings, goals, and tasks.

The demands of young children do subside eventually, as we note in Chapter 3, but before a couple can celebrate the advent of the postparental period, they may be forced to adjust to a nest that will not empty or is refilled occasionally. Departures, arrivals, and extended stays by grown children can have a significant effect on the temporal, financial, and emotional resources of older parents. Where there has been a warm and mutually supportive couple relationship, the family is most likely to weather these changes with a minimum of discord and without relationships becoming detached.

Although the spare bedroom in the nest may still occasionally be in use, a couple may find themselves having to adjust to the new role of grandparents. The literature discussed in Chapter 4 underscores the wide variety of responses that couples may have to this development. If grandparenthood is "on-time" and the situation acceptable (i.e., the adult child is in a stable marriage), the transition appears welcome and satisfying. Any negotiation that occurs between the new grandmother and grandfather seems to involve how much time will be spent being active in the role. As we have seen from the Ryans' case earlier in this chapter, there may be marked sex differences, but typically some compromise is reached. On the other hand, if grandparenthood is too early or late, or involves an unexpected situation such as the blending of families, the couple may find it difficult to accept the new role. Nevertheless, it does appear that attachment to their adult children, and commitment to the future of the family, help older couples adapt to even the most unusual situations.

While intensely involved in the marital and parent–child relationships, couples still manage to maintain their bonds to siblings. As the research discussed in Chapter 5 suggests, attachment to siblings may remain strong from childhood through old age, even though the degree and kind of contact changes. Early in life, when sibling rivalries are strongest, identity relations are sustained through bonds to parents and the family of origin. Later, when childhood conflicts have been outgrown, attachment feelings may strengthen and siblings provide companionship and support for one another. As we have seen, however, the family context for sibling relationships is extremely important. If one member of a marital couple discourages interaction with the spouse's brothers and sisters, attachment feelings may remain, but attachment behaviors may be extremely limited.

The influence of a spouse on the social interaction of the couple can also be seen in the literature on friendship discussed in Chapter 6. Men and women bring individual friendships with them when they marry, some of which will not survive the new situation. As we have seen, family circumstances have a marked impact on the kind of friends couples choose and maintain. During the period of active parenting, for example, childless friends may be neglected in favor of those with whom couples can exchange advice and baby-sitting. During this period, a kind of generalized norm of reciprocity seems to prevail. Later in life, however, couples seem more concerned with immediate repayment of support received, especially from new friends. Couples who have a strong, supportive relationship with each other are likely to weather successfully changing friendships and friendship needs.

What Was Not Covered

In this book, we have focused on the couple's journey through varying and changing relationships. Because of this life-span perspective, married couples who stay together long enough to experience parenthood and grandparenthood, to collect longtime friends, and to experience lengthy relationships with extended kin have been the focus. Wherever possible, we have noted the differing experiences of single parents, reconstituted families, and those in other nontraditional families. Nevertheless, there are some family forms, such as lesbian parents, for which there is no extant gerontology literature and precious little dealing with intergenerational relationships.

We have included available information about cultural and ethnic variations. There is, however, very little to go on. Most research has used convenient samples: well-educated, white, middle-class North Americans. Where ethnic and racial minority research does exist, it does not begin to reflect the diverse racial and ethnic groupings living in North America. Similarly, the subject material covered is very limited, thereby precluding comprehensive analyses.

Despite this limitation, the conceptual framework employed in this book is likely to have explanatory power across varying family types and situations. Attachment in childhood has been conceptualized as having a strong biological component (Bowlby, 1969). Recently, other researchers have argued that adult love is a mature form of attachment that still maintains its evolutionary roots (Hazan & Shaver, 1987). If this is the case, attachment feelings between spouses, children, and the other significant people in their lives should occur across situations and cultures, although their expression may differ (Ikels, 1988). Clearly, future study should be directed toward such possible differences.

It is also likely that the need and the desire to exchange intrafamilial support transcend cultures and situations. Some researchers have noted that, regardless of ethnic group, older people prefer "intimacy at a distance"—having close and supportive interactions with their children and extended family but living independently—as a strategy for managing intergenerational relationships (Driedger & Chappell, 1987). There is some research to suggest that the degree of assistance exchanged among family members may differ by ethnic group: For example, in Canada older parents of Chinese or Dutch descent are more likely to share a residence with their children than those of English or French extraction (Driedger & Chappell, 1987). Whether these patterns reflect differences in norms of helping and reciprocity across ethnic and cultural groups is not at all clear. Perhaps practical concerns are more important. It may be that some ethnic elderly, particularly recent immigrants, live with their children because they lack the financial resources for a separate residence or because they are not familiar with the language of their adopted country. Once again, more research is needed to explore the differing expression that reciprocal support within families may take.

Where Do We Go from Here?

Parents trying to come to grips with adult children refilling the nest is a recurrent theme in the popular press. People approaching what we used to think of as the "empty nest" period in the family life cycle clearly want to understand the changing relationships between themselves and their spouses, family members, and friends. They are interested in the influence on their interactions of individual development, family life cycle stage, and the social-historical context. Even more urgent appears to be the need for advice on how to adjust their relationships with others to weather such influences. For example, a recent issue of a magazine for parents featured an article entitled "Friends Again: When Sisters Become Moms" (Stone, 1992).The article suggested that siblings may remain rivals until they have children of their own. At this time, they have two choices: repeating the mistakes of their childhood—for example, by competing about whose child is the smartest—or repairing the relationship through mutual support. The keys to turning a rival sibling into an ally, according to the author, are communicating openly about the current relationship and leaving past resentments behind.

This strategy sounds reasonable, and the author supports it with comments by family therapists and academics. Nevertheless, no research findings are reported. There are two reasons for this: One of these is a lack of relevant research; the other is a lack of effort by researchers to make their work accessible to the public and by writers of popular books to acknowledge existing research. First, it is difficult to find answers to "family problems" within the scholarly literature because so little of it focuses on the intergenerational family as it moves through the life course. To restate a point made earlier in this chapter, most studies choose an isolated period in the life span, for example, the grandparental years, and focus on an individual's response to this period. It may be of interest to academics that many grandparents are "formal" in their style, but an older couple is not likely to find that useful in negotiating their relationships with their grandchildren. Instead, they are likely to buy *How to Grandparent* (Dodson, 1981), a volume full of practical tips on how to handle visits and what type of toys to buy, but lacking a research base.

Nevertheless, there *is* information in the scholarly literature that may be helpful to aging couples. It is up to all researchers to make their work more visible, and to make the practical application of research findings clearer to the lay reader. This book was written with these goals in mind. As researchers, we wanted to apply some of our own data in new contexts, comment on the available literature, and suggest avenues for future work; as family members, we wanted to provide insights into the intergenerational relationships that all of us manage as we move through our lives. Through a focus on attachment and support, we have provided a means for family members to understand each other's feelings and behaviors. Through our emphasis on negotiation, specifically tailored to different types of relationships, we have suggested an avenue for coping with changes in these relationships as well as promoting growth. We hope that our ideas will enrich family members' understanding of their relationships, and inspire family researchers to ask further questions about how these relationships evolve across the family life cycle, among generations.

References

Adams, B. (1968). *Kinship in an urban setting*. Chicago: Markham.

Adams, R. G., & Blieszner, R. (Eds.). (1989). *Older adult friendship: Structure and process*. Newbury Park, Calif.: Sage.

Aldous, J. (1985). Parent–child relations as affected by the grandparent status. In V. L. Bengtson & J. F. Robertson (Eds.), *Grandparenthood*. Beverly Hills, Calif.: Sage.

Allen, G. A., & Adams, R. G. (1989). Aging and the structure of friendship. In R. G. Adams & R. Blieszner (Eds.), *Older adult friendship: Structure and process* (pp. 45–64). Newbury Park, Calif.: Sage.

Antonucci, T. C. (1976). Attachment: A life-span concept. *Human Development, 19*, 135–142.

Aquilino, W. S. (1990). The likelihood of parent–adult child coresidence: Effects of family structure and parental characteristics. *Journal of Marriage and the Family, 52*, 405–419.

Aquilino, W. S., & Supple, K. R. (1991). Parent–child relations and parent's satisfaction with living arrangements when adult children live at home. *Journal of Marriage and the Family, 53*, 13–27.

Argyle, M., & Henderson, M. (1984). The rules of friendship. *Journal of Social and Personal Relationships, 1*, 211–237.

Avioli, P. S. (1989). The social support functions of siblings in later life: A theoretical model. *American Behavioral Scientist, 33*, 45–57.

Baltes, P. B. (1979). Life-span developmental psychology: Some converging observations on history and theory. In P. B. Baltes & O. G. Brim (Eds.), *Life-span development and behavior*, Vol. 2, (pp. 255–279). New York: Academic Press.

Baltes, P. B., Reese, H. W., & Lipsitt, L. P. (1980). Life-span developmental psychology. *Annual Review of Psychology, 31*, 65–110.

Bank, D., & Kahn, M. D. (1975). Sisterhood–brotherhood is powerful: Sibling subsystems and family therapy. *Family Process, 14*, 311–337.

Bank, S. P., & Kahn, M. D. (1982). *The sibling bond*. New York: Basic.

Barnett, R. C., & Baruch, G. K. (1985). Women's involvement in multiple roles and psychological distress. *Journal of Personality and Social Psychology, 49*, 135–145.

Barranti, C. C. R. (1985). The grandparent/grandchild relationship: Family resource in an era of voluntary bonds. *Family Relations, 34*, 343–352.

Bedford, V. H. (1989a). Ambivalence in adult sibling relationships. *Journal of Family Issues, 10*, 211–224.

Bedford, V. H. (1989b). Sibling research in historical perspective. *American Behavioral Scientist, 33*, 6–18.

Bedford, V. H. (1989c). Understanding the value of siblings in old age. *American Behavioral Scientist, 33*, 33–44.

Bedford, V. H. (1992). Memories of parental favoritism and the quality of parent–child ties in adulthood. *Journal of Gerontology, 47*, S149–155.

Belsky, J., & Pensky, E. (1988). Marital change across the transition to parenthood. *Marriage and Family Review*, *12*, 133–156.

Belsky, J., & Rovine, M. (1990). Patterns of marital change across the transition to parenthood: Pregnancy to three years postpartum. *Journal of Marriage and the Family*, *52*, 5–19.

Bengtson, V., & Kuypers, J. A. (1971). Generational differences and the developmental stake. *Aging and Human Development*, *2*, 246–260.

Berger, P. L., & Kellner, H. (1970). Marriage and the construction of reality. In H. P. Dreitzel (Ed.), *Recent sociology*, No. 2 (pp. 49–72). New York: Macmillan.

Berman, H. J. (1987). Adult children and their parents: Irredeemable obligation and irreplaceable loss. *Journal of Gerontological Social Work*, *10*, 21–34.

Blake, J., Richardson, B., & Bhattacharya, J. (1991). Number of siblings and sociability. *Journal of Marriage and the Family*, *53*, 271–283.

Blau, Z. (1981). *Aging in a changing society* (2nd ed.). New York: Franklin Watts.

Blieszner, R. (1989). An agenda for future research on friendships of older adults. In R. G. Adams & R. Blieszner (Eds.), *Older adult friendship: Structure and process* (pp. 245–252). Newbury Park, Calif.: Sage.

Blieszner, R., & Mancini, J. (1987). Enduring ties: Older adults' parental role and responsibilities. *Family Relations*, *36*, 176–180.

Bohannon, P. (1970). The six stages of divorce. In P. Bohannon (Ed.), *Divorce and after*. New York: Doubleday.

Bond, J. B., Jr., Harvey, C. D. H., & Greenwood, L. J. (1991, October). *Support to older parents in rural Men-* *nonite and Non-Mennonite settings.* Paper presented at the annual meeting of the Canadian Association on Gerontology, Toronto, Ontario.

Bowlby, J. (1969). *Attachment and loss, Vol. I: Attachment.* New York: Basic.

Bowlby, J. (1973). *Attachment and loss, Vol. II: Separation.* New York: Basic.

Bowlby, J. (1980). *Attachment and loss, Vol. III: Loss, Sadness and Depression.* New York: Basic.

Boyd, M., & Pryor, E. T. (1989). The cluttered nest: The living arrangements of young Canadian adults. *Canadian Journal of Sociology*, *14*, 461–477.

Brenton, M. (1974). *Friendship*. Briarcliff Manor, N.Y.: Stein & Day.

Brody, E. (1985). *Mental and physical health practices of older people*. New York: Springer.

Brody, E. M., Hoffman, C., Kleban, M. H., & Schoonover, C. B. (1989). Caregiving daughters and their local siblings: Perceptions, strains, and interactions. *Gerontologist*, *29*, 529–538.

Burch, T. K. (1981, December). *Interactive decision making in the determination of residence patterns and family relations.* Paper presented at the International Population Conference, International Union for the Scientific Study of Population, Manila.

Burton, L. M., & Bengtson, V. L. (1985). Black grandmothers: Issues of timing and continuity in roles. In V. L. Bengtson & J. F. Robertson (Eds.), *Grandparenthood* (pp. 61–77). Beverly Hills, Calif.: Sage.

Calzavara, L. (1988). Trends and policy in employment opportunities for women. In J. Curtis, E. Grabb, N. Guppy, & S. Gilbert (Eds.), *Social inequality in Canada: Patterns, problems, policies* (pp. 287–299). Scarborough, Ontario: Prentice-Hall.

Canada's birth rate rises for third year. (1992, March 31). *Kitchener-Waterloo Record*, pp. A1–2.

Canadian Press (1991, December 17). Statistics Canada data. *Kitchener-Waterloo Record*.

Canadian Press (1992, December 26). Statistics Canada data. *Guelph Mercury*.

Canadian Press (1993, January 6). Multiple births up, study says. *Kitchener-Waterloo Record*, p. A3.

Carter, L. (1990). *Congratulations! You're going to be a grandmother*. New York: Pocket Books.

Cassidy, M. (1985). Role conflict in the postparental period: The effects of employment status on the marital satisfaction of women. *Research on Aging*, 7, 433–454.

Catalyst staff (1988). Workplace policies: New options for fathers. In P. Bronstein & C. P. Cowan (Eds.), *Fatherhood today: Men's changing role in the family* (pp. 323–340). New York: John Wiley & Sons.

Cavanaugh, J. C. (1990). *Adult development and aging*. Belmont, Calif.: Wadsworth.

Chappell, N. L. (1991). *Social support and aging*. Toronto: Butterworths.

Chen, A. B. (1992, October). *Attitudes toward grandparents: A cross-cultural comparison*. Paper presented at the annual meeting of the Canadian Association on Gerontology, Edmonton, Alberta.

Chilman, C. S. (1981). *Remarriage and stepfamilies: An overview of research, observations, and some implications for further study and program development*. Paper presented at the annual meeting of the Groves Conference on Marriage and the Family.

Cicirelli, V. G. (1980a). A comparison of college women's feelings towards their siblings and parents. *Journal of Marriage and the Family*, 42, 111–120.

Cicirelli, V. G. (1980b). Sibling relationships in adulthood: A life-span perspective. In L. W. Poon (Ed.), *Aging in the 1980s* (pp. 455–462). Washington, D.C.: American Psychological Association.

Cicirelli, V. G. (1983a). Adult children and their elderly parents. In T. Brubaker (Ed.), *Family relationships in later life* (pp. 31–46). Beverly Hills, Calif.: Sage.

Cicirelli, V. G. (1983b). Adult children's attachment and helping behavior to elderly parents: A path model. *Journal of Marriage and the Family*, 45, 815–824.

Cicirelli, V. G. (1989). Feelings of attachment to siblings and well-being in later life. *Psychology and Aging*, 4, 211–216.

Cicirelli, V. G. (1991a). Attachment theory in old age: Protection of the attached figure. In K. Pillemer & K. McCartney (Eds.), *Parent-child relations throughout life* (pp. 25–42). Hillsdale, N.J.: Erlbaum.

Cicirelli, V. G. (1991b). Sibling relationships in adulthood. *Marriage and Family Review*, 16, 291–310.

Clemens, A. W., & Axelson, L. (1985). The not-so-empty nest: The return of the fledgling adult. *Family Relations*, 34, 259–264.

Cleveland, W. P., & Gianturco, D. T. (1976). Remarriage probability after widowhood: A retrospective method. *Journal of Gerontology*, 31, 99–103.

Clouthier, K. (1986). *Influence of family of origin and marital dyad upon father involvement in parenting activity*. Unpublished master's thesis, University of Guelph, Guelph, Ontario.

Connidis, I. A. (1989a). Contact between siblings in later life. *Canadian Journal of Sociology, 14*, 429–442.

Connidis, I. A. (1989b). *Family ties and aging.* Toronto: Butterworths.

Connidis, I. A. (1989c). Siblings as friends in later life. *American Behavioral Scientist, 33*, 81–93.

Connidis, I. A. (1991). *Sibling ties and life transitions.* Paper presented to the Gerontology Research Centre Seminar Series, University of Guelph, Guelph, Ontario.

Connidis, I., & Davies, L. (1990). Confidants and companions in later life: The place of family and friends. *Journal of Gerontology, 45*, S141–149.

Cooper, C., Grotevant, H., & Condon, S. (1983). Individuality and connectedness in the family as a context for adolescent identity formation and role-taking skill. In H. Grotevant & C. Cooper (Eds.), *Adolescent development in the family: New directions for child development*, No. 22, (pp. 43–59). San Francisco: Jossey-Bass.

Cooper, K. L., & Gutman, D. L. (1987). Gender identity and ego mastery style in middle-aged, pre- and post-empty nest women. *Gerontologist, 27*, 347–352.

Cowan, C. P., & Bronstein, P. (1988). Father's role in the family: Implications for research, intervention and change. In P. Bronstein & C. P. Cowan (Eds.), *Fatherhood today: Men's changing role in the family* (pp. 341–347). New York: John Wiley and Sons.

Cowan, C. P., & Cowan, P. A. (1992). *When partners become parents: The big life change for couples.* New York: Basic Books.

Cowan, C. P., Cowan, P. A., Heming, G., Coysh, W. S., Curtis-Bowles, H., & Bowles, A. J. (1985). Transition to parenthood: His, hers, and theirs. *Journal of Family Issues, 6*, 543–564.

Cox, F. D. (1990). *Human intimacy: Marriage, the family and its meaning* (5th ed.). St. Paul, Minn.: West Publishing.

Creighton, J. (1993, March 13). Social worker tries to bridge the gap. *Kitchener-Waterloo Record*, p. G2.

Cunningham-Burley, S. (1986). Becoming a grandparent. *Ageing and Society, 6*, 453–470.

Daly, K. (1992). Parenthood as problematic: Insider interviews with couples seeking to adopt. In J. F. Gilgun, K. Daly, & G. Handel (Eds.), *Qualitative methods in family research* (pp. 103–125). Newbury Park, Calif.: Sage.

Day, A. T. (1985). *"We can manage": Expectations about care and varieties of family support among people 75 years and over.* Melbourne, Australia: Institute of Family Studies.

Demo, D. H., Small, S. A., & Savin-Williams, R. C. (1987). Family relations and the self-esteem of adolescents and their parents. *Journal of Marriage and the Family, 49*, 705–715.

Denham, T. E., & Smith, C. W. (1989). The influence of grandparents on grandchildren: A review of the literature and resources. *Family Relations, 38*, 345–350.

Depner, C., & Ingersoll-Dayton, B. (1985). Conjugal social support: Patterns in later life. *Journal of Gerontology, 40*, 761–766.

Dodson, F., with Reuben, P. (1981). *How to grandparent.* New York: Signet New American Library.

Doka, K. J., & Mertz, M. (1988). The meaning and significance of great-grandparenthood. *Gerontologist, 28*, 192–197.

Dolen, L. (1992, November 7). Parents can rescue their children from the negative equity trap. *Times* (London), p. 32.

Dowd, J. (1975). Aging as exchange: A preface to a theory. *Journal of Gerontology, 30*, 584–594.

Dowd, J. J. (1980). *Stratification among the aged.* Pacific Grove, Calif.: Brooks-Cole.

Driedger, L., & Chappell, N. (1987). *Aging and ethnicity: Toward an interface.* Toronto: Butterworths.

Dunn, J. (1991). The developmental importance of differences in siblings' experience within the family. In K. Pillemer & K. McCarthey (Eds.), *Parentchild relations throughout life* (pp. 113–124). Hillsdale, N.J.: Erlbaum.

Dunn, J., & Plomin, R. (1991). Why are siblings so different? The significance of differences in sibling experiences with the family. *Family Process, 30*, 271–283.

Edwards, J. N., & Demo, D. H. (1991). *Marriage and family in transition.* Boston: Allyn & Bacon.

Eggebeen, D. J., & Hogan, D. P. (1990). Giving between generations in American families. *Human Nature, 1*, 211–232.

Eisenhandler, S. (1992). Lifelong roles and cameo appearances: Elderly parents and relationships with adult children. *Journal of Aging Studies, 6*, 243–257.

Fennel, T., Luckow, D., Daly, J., & Jenish, D. (1988, August 15). Beyond reach. *Maclean's*, pp. 24–27.

Fine, M. (1991, May). Personal communication.

Fine, M., & Norris, J. E. (1989). Intergenerational relations and family therapy research: What we can learn from other disciplines. *Family Process, 28*, 1–5.

Fine, M. A., McKenry, P. C., Donnelly, B. W., & Voydanoff, P. (1992). Perceived adjustment of parents and children: Variations by family structure, race and gender. *Journal of Marriage and the Family, 54*, 118–127.

Fischer, C. S., & Oliker, S. J. (1983). A research note on friendship, gender and the life cycle. *Social Forces, 62*, 124–133.

Fischer, L. R. (1981). Transitions in the mother-daughter relationship. *Journal of Marriage and the Family, 43*, 613–622.

Fischer, L. R. (1986). *Linked lives: Adult daughters and their mothers.* New York: Harper & Row.

Fischer, L. R. (1988). The influence of kin on the transition to parenthood. *Marriage and Family Review, 12*, 201–219.

Fisher, C. B., Reid, J. D., & Melendez, M. (1989). Conflict in families and friendships of later life. *Family Relations, 38*, 83–89.

Fisher, H. E. (1987). *Growing old in America.* New York: Oxford University Press.

Fitzpatrick, M. A. (1984). A topological approach to marital interaction: Recent theory and research. *Advances in Experimental Sociology, 18*, 1–47.

Fredrickson, B. L., & Carstensen, L. L. (1990). Choosing social partners: How old age and anticipated endings make people more selective. *Psychology and Aging, 5*, 335–347.

Gecas, V., & Seff, M. A. (1990). Families and adolescents: A review of the 1980s. *Journal of Marriage and the Family, 52*, 941–958.

Gee, E. M. (1991). The transition to grandmotherhood: A quantitative study. *Canadian Journal on Aging, 10*, 254–270.

Gee, E. M., & Kimball, M. M. (1987). *Women and aging.* Toronto: Butterworths.

Gentry, M., & Shulman, A. D. (1988). Remarriage as a coping response for widowhood. *Psychology and Aging, 3,* 191–196.

Getting married affects friends. (1990, January 24). *Guelph Tribune,* p. B9

Gladstone, J. W. (1987a). *A study of grandparents whose children have remarried following divorce.* Publication Series Paper No. 87-4. Guelph, Ontario: Gerontology Research Centre, University of Guelph.

Gladstone, J. W. (1987b). Factors associated with the changes in visiting between grandmothers and grandchildren following an adult child's marriage breakdown. *Canadian Journal on Aging, 6,* 117–127.

Gladstone, J. W. (1988). Perceived changes in grandmother–grandchild relations following a child's separation or divorce. *Gerontologist, 28,* 66–72.

Gladstone, J. W. (1989). Grandmother–grandchild contact: The mediating influence of the middle generation following marriage breakdown and remarriage. *Canadian Journal on Aging, 8,* 355–365.

Gladstone, J. W. (1991). An analysis of changes in grandparent–grandchild visitation following an adult child's remarriage. *Canadian Journal on Aging, 10,* 113–126.

Glick, P. C., & Lin, S. L. (1986). More young adults are living with their parents: Who are they? *Journal of Marriage and the Family, 48,* 107–112.

Goetting, A. (1986). The developmental tasks of siblingship over the life cycle. *Journal of Marriage and the Family, 48,* 703–714.

Gold, D. T. (1987). Siblings in old age: Something special. *Canadian Journal on Aging, 6,* 199–215.

Gold, D. T. (1989a). Sibling relationships in old age: A typology. *International Journal of Aging and Human Development, 28,* 37–51.

Gold, D. T. (1989b). Generational solidarity: Conceptual antecedents and consequences. *American Behavioral Scientist, 33,* 19–32.

Gold, D. T., Woodbury, M. A., & George, L. K. (1990). Relationship classification using grade of membership analysis: A typology of sibling relationships in later life. *Journal of Gerontology, 45,* S43–51.

Goldscheider, F. K., & DaVanzo, J. (1986). Semiautonomy and transition to adulthood. *Social Forces, 65,* 187–201.

Goldscheider, F. K., & Goldscheider, C. (1991). The intergenerational flow of income: Family structure and the status of black Americans. *Journal of Marriage and the Family, 53,* 499–508.

Gottlieb, B. H. (1983). Social support as a focus for integrative research in psychology. *American Psychologist, 38,* 278–287.

Gouldner, A. J. (1967). Reciprocity and autonomy in functional theory. In N. J. Demerath III & R. A. Peterson (Eds.), *System, change and conflict* (pp. 141–169). New York: Free Press.

Graham, S. (1992). "Most of the subjects were white and middle class." Trends in published research on African-Americans in selected APA journals, 1970–1989. *American Psychologist, 47,* 629–639.

Greenberg, J. S., & Becker, M. (1988). Aging parents as family resources. *Gerontologist, 28,* 786–791.

Gutmann, D. (1978). *Personal transformation in the post-parental period: A cross-cultural view.* Washington, D.C.: American Association for the Advancement of Science.

Hagestad, G. O. (1981). Problems and promises in the social psychology of intergenerational relations. In R. W. Fogel, E. Hatfield, S. B. Kiesler, & E. Shanas (Eds.), *Aging: Stability and change in the family* (pp. 11–46). New York: Academic Press.

Hagestad, G. O. (1985). Generations: Family and history. In V. L. Bengtson & J. F. Robertson (Eds.), *Grandparenthood.* Beverly Hills, Calif.: Sage.

Hagestad, G. O. (1987). Parent–child relations in later life: Trends and gaps in past research. In J. B. Lancaster, J. Altmann, A. S. Rossi, & L. R. Sherrod (Eds.), *Parenting across the life span: Biosocial dimensions* (pp. 405–433). New York: Aldine de Gruyter.

Hagestad, G. O., & Lang, M. E. (1986). The transition to grandparenthood: Unexplored issues. *Journal of Family Issues, 7,* 115–130.

Hareven, T. (1987). Historical analysis of the family. In M. Sussman & S. Steinmetz (Eds.), *Handbook of marriage and the family* (pp. 37–57). New York: Plenum.

Hatch, L. R., & Bulcroft, K. (1992). Contact with friends in later life: Disentangling the effects of gender and marital status. *Journal of Marriage and the Family, 54,* 222–232.

Havemann, E., & Lehtinen, M. (1990). *Marriages and families: New problems, new opportunities.* Englewood Cliffs, N.J.: Prentice-Hall.

Hazan, C., & Shaver, P. (1987). Romantic love conceptualized as an attachment process. *Journal of Personality and Social Psychology, 52,* 511–524.

Hess, B. B. (1989). Foreward. In R. G. Adams & R. Blieszner (Eds.), *Older adult friendship: Structure and process* (pp. 7–9). Newbury Park, Calif.: Sage.

Hochschild, A. R., & Machung, A. (1989). *The second shift: Working parents and the revolution at home.* New York: Viking.

Horowitz, A. (1985). Sons and daughters as caregivers to older parents: Differences in role performance and consequences. *Gerontologist, 25,* 612–617.

Huston, T. L., McHale, S. M., & Crouter, A. C. (1986). When the honeymoon's over: Changes in the relationship over the first year. In R. Gilmour & S. Duck (Eds.), *The emerging field of personal relationships* (pp. 109–132). Hillsdale, N.J.: Erlbaum.

Ikels, C. (1988). Delayed reciprocity and support networks of the childless elderly. *Journal of Comparative Family Studies, 19,* 99–112.

Ilse, S. (1982). *Empty arms.* Long Lake, Minn.: Wintergreen Press.

Ingersoll-Dayton, B., & Antonucci, T. C. (1988). Reciprocal and nonreciprocal social support: Contrasting sides of intimate relationships. *Journal of Gerontology, 43,* 565–573.

Joe, S. (1991, October 31). Many children "boomerang" to parents' house as adults. *Kitchener-Waterloo Record,* p. F5.

Johnson, C. L. (1985). Grandparenting options in divorcing families: An anthropological perspective. In V. L. Bengtson & J. F. Robertson (Eds.), *Grandparenthood.* Beverly Hills, Calif.: Sage.

Jones, D. C., & Vaughn, K. (1990). Close friendships among senior adults. *Psychology and Aging, 5,* 451–457.

Kahana, E., Midlarsky, E., & Kahana, B. (1987). Beyond dependency, autonomy, and exchange: Prosocial behavior in late-life adaptation. *Social Justice and Research, 1,* 439–459.

Kennedy, G. E. (1990). College students' expectations of grandparent and grandchild role behaviors. *Gerontologist, 30,* 43–45.

Kingson, E., Hirshorn, B., & Cornman, J. (1986). *Ties that bind: The interdependence of generations.* Washington, D.C.: Seven Locks Press.

Kinsella, E. (1986). Can you make it to the top and still be a good mother? In F. W. Burck (Ed.), *Mothers talking: Sharing the secret* (pp. 187–192). New York: St. Martin's Press.

Kivett, V. R. (1985). Grandfathers and grandchildren: Patterns of association, helping, and psychological closeness. *Family Relations, 34,* 565–571.

Kivnick, H. Q. (1981). Grandparenthood and the mental health of grandparents. *Aging and Society, 1,* 365–392.

Kivnick, H. Q. (1988). Grandparenthood, life review, and psychosocial development. *Journal of Gerontological Social Work, 12,* 63–81.

Klagsbrun, F. (1992). *Mixed feelings: Love, hate, rivalry and reconciliation among brothers and sisters.* New York: Bantam.

Knudsen, N. K. (1988). *Cross-sex friendships in later life.* Unpublished master's thesis, University of Guelph, Guelph, Ontario.

Kornhaber, A. (1985). Grandparenthood and the "new social contract." In V. L. Bengtson & J. F. Robertson (Eds.), *Grandparenthood.* Beverly Hills, Calif.: Sage.

Kornhaber, A., & Woodward, K. L. (1981). *Grandparents/grandchild: The vital connection.* Garden City, N.Y.: Anchor.

Krier, B. A. (1992, February 14). Sisters forge strongest bonds among siblings. *Kitchener-Waterloo Record,* p. E1.

LaFreniere, P. J., & Sroufe, L. A. (1985). Profiles of peer competence in the preschool: Interrelationships between measures, influence of social ecology, and relation to attachment history. *Developmental Psychology, 21,* 56–69.

Lamanna, M. A., & Reidmann, A. (1988). *Marriages and families: Making choices and facing change* (3rd ed.). Belmont, Calif.: Wadsworth.

Lamb, M. E., & Sutton-Smith, B. (Eds.). (1982). *Sibling relationships: Their nature and significance across the lifespan.* Hillsdale, N.J.: Erlbaum.

Landers, A. (1991, May). *Kitchener-Waterloo Record.*

Langer, N. (1990). Grandparents and adult grandchildren: What do they do for one another? *International Journal of Aging and Human Development, 31,* 101–110.

Larsen, D. (1990, December/1991, January). Unplanned parenthood. *Modern Maturity,* pp. 32–36.

Laslett, P. (1971). *The world we have lost.* London: Methuen.

Lasswell, M., & Lasswell, T. (1991). *Marriage and the family* (3rd ed.). Belmont, Calif.: Wadsworth.

Lee, T. R., Mancini, J. A., & Maxwell, J. W. (1990). Sibling relationships in adulthood: Contact patterns and motivations. *Journal of Marriage and the Family, 52,* 431–440.

Lerner, M. J. (1981). The justice motive in human relations: Some thoughts on what we know and need to know about justice. In M. J. Lerner &

S. C. Lerner (Eds.), *The justice motive in social behavior: Adapting to times of scarcity and change* (pp. 11–35). New York: Plenum.

Lerner, M. J., Somers, D. G., Reid, D., Chiriboga, D., & Tierney, M. (1991). Adult children as caregivers: Egocentric biases in judgments of sibling contributions. *Gerontologist, 31,* 746–755.

Lerner, M. J., Somers, D. G., Reid, D., & Tierney, M. (1988). The social psychology of individual and social dilemmas: Egocentrically biased cognitions among filial caregivers. In S. Spacapan & S. Oskamp (Eds.), *The social psychology of aging: Claremont Symposium on Applied Social Psychology.* Newbury Park, Calif.: Sage.

Leroy, M. (1988). *Miscarriage.* London: Macdonald.

Lewis, R. A. (1990). The adult child and older parents. In T. H. Brubaker (Ed.), *Family relationships in later life* (2nd ed., pp. 68–85). Newbury Park, Calif.: Sage.

Litwak, E. (1989). Forms of friendships among older people in an industrial society. In R. G. Adams & R. Blieszner (Eds.), *Older adult friendship: Structure and process* (pp. 65–88). Newbury Park, Calif.: Sage.

Lopata, H. Z. (1979). *Women as widows.* New York: Elsevier.

Lowenthal, M., Thurner, M., & Chiriboga, D. (1975). *Four stages of life.* San Francisco: Jossey-Bass.

Lupri, E., & Frideres, J. (1981). The quality of marriage and the passage of time: Marital satisfaction over the family life cycle. *Canadian Journal of Sociology, 6,* 283–305.

Mac Rae, H. (1992). Fictive kin as a component of the social networks of older people. *Research on Aging, 14,* 226–247.

Mallinckrodt, B. (1992). Childhood emotional bonds with parents, development of adult social competencies, and availability of social support. *Journal of Counseling Psychology, 39,* 453–461.

Mancini, J. A., & Blieszner, R. (1985). Return of middle-aged children to the parental home. *Medical Aspects of Human Sexuality, 19,* 192–194.

Mancini, J. A., & Blieszner, R. (1989). Aging parents and adult children: Research themes in intergenerational relations. *Journal of Marriage and the Family, 51,* 275–290.

Marcil-Gratton, N., & Legare, J. (1992). Will reduced fertility lead to greater isolation in old age for tomorrow's elderly? *Canadian Journal on Aging, 11,* 54–71.

Markides, K. S., Liang, J., & Jackson, J. S. (1990). Race, ethnicity, and aging: Conceptual and methodological issues. In R. H. Binstock & L. K. George (Eds.), *Handbook of aging and the social sciences* (3rd ed., pp. 112–129). San Diego: Academic Press.

Markstrom-Adams, C. (1991). Attitudes on dating, courtship, and marriage: Perspectives on in-group versus out-group relations by religious minority and majority adolescents. *Family Relations, 40,* 91–96.

Martin Matthews, A. (1987). Widowhood as an expectable life event. In V. W. Marshall (Ed.), *Aging in Canada: Social perspectives* (2nd ed., pp. 343–366). Toronto: Fitzhenry & Whiteside.

Martin Matthews, A. (1991) *Widowhood in later life.* Toronto: Butterworths.

Martin Matthews, A. (1992). *Rural-urban comparisons of the social supports of the widowed elderly* (final report to Social Sciences and Humanities Research Council of

Canada Project No. 492-84-0020). Guelph, Ontario: University of Guelph.

Matras, J. (1990). *Dependency, obligations, and entitlements: A new sociology of aging, the life course, and the elderly.* Englewood Cliffs, N.J.: Prentice-Hall.

Matthews, R., & Martin Matthews, A. (1986). Infertility and involuntary childlessness: The transition to nonparenthood. *Journal of Marriage and the Family, 48,* 641–649.

Matthews, S. H. (1986). *Friendships through the life course.* Beverly Hills, Calif.: Sage.

Matthews, S. H. (1987). Perceptions of fairness in the division of responsibility for old parents. *Social Justice Research, 4,* 425–438.

Matthews, S. H., Delaney, P. J., & Adamek, M. E. (1989). Male kinship ties: Bonds between adult brothers. *American Behavioral Scientist, 33,* 58–69.

Matthews, S. H., & Sprey, J. (1984). The impact of divorce on grandparenthood: An exploratory study. *Gerontologist, 24,* 41–47.

McAdoo, J. L. (1988). Changing perspectives on the role of the black father. In P. Bronstein & C. P. Cowan (Eds.), *Fatherhood today: Men's changing role in the family* (pp. 79–92). New York: John Wiley and Sons.

McCullough, B. J. (1990). The relationship of intergenerational reciprocity of aid to the morale of older parents: Equity and exchange theory comparisons. *Journal of Gerontology, 45,* S150–155.

McDaniel, S. (1986). *Canada's aging population.* Toronto: Butterworths.

McDonald, G. W., & Osmond, M. W. (1980). *Jealousy and trust: Unexplored dimensions of social exchange*

dynamics. Paper presented at the annual meeting of the National Council on Family Relations.

McGhee, J. L. (1985). The effects of siblings on the life satisfaction of the rural elderly. *Journal of Marriage and the Family, 48,* 703–714.

McGreal, C. E. (1983, August). *Transition to grandparenthood: Significance of the role to "expectant" grandparents.* Paper presented at the annual convention of the American Psychological Association, Anaheim, Calif.

McGreal, C. E. (1986). Grandparental role-meaning types: A critical evaluation. *Infant Mental Health Journal, 7,* 235–241.

Mead, M. (1972). *Blackberry winter: A memoir.* New York: William Morrow.

Mebert, C. J. (1991). Variability in the transition to parenthood experience. In K. Pillemer & K. McCartney (Eds.), *Parent–child relations throughout life* (pp. 43–57). Hillsdale, N.J.: Erlbaum.

Mills, J., & Clark, M. S. (1982). Exchange and communal relationships. In L. Wheeler (Ed.), *Review of personality and social psychology.* Beverly Hills, Calif.: Sage.

Mindel, C. H., & Habenstein, R. W. (Eds.). (1981). *Ethnic families in America: Patterns and variations* (2nd ed.). New York: Elsevier.

Morris, J. N., & Sherwood, S. (1984). Informal support resources for vulnerable elderly persons: Can they be counted on, why do they work? *International Journal of Aging and Human Development, 18,* 1–17.

Moss, M. S., & Moss, S. Z. (1992). Themes in parentchild relationships when parents move nearby. *Journal of Aging Studies, 6,* 259–271.

Moss, S. Z., & Moss, M. S. (1989). The impact of the death of an elderly sibling. *American Behavioral Scientist, 33,* 94–106.

Nett, E. M. (1988). *Canadian families: Past and present.* Toronto: Butterworths.

Neugarten, B. L., & Weinstein, K. K. (1964). The changing American grandparent. *Journal of Marriage and the Family, 26,* 199–204.

Norris, J. E. (1978). [Social disengagement in young and old adults.] Unpublished raw data.

Norris, J. E. (1981). [The careers of successful older professionals.] Unpublished raw data.

Norris, J. E. (1986). Grandparenting relations. *Proceedings of the Conference on Intergenerational Relationships and Programming.* Guelph, Ontario: Gerontology Research Centre, University of Guelph.

Norris, J. E. (1987a). Grandparenting relationships: Implications for intergenerational programming. *Proceedings of the Intergenerational Relations and Programming Conference.* Guelph, Ontario: Gerontology Research Centre, University of Guelph.

Norris, J. E. (1987b). Psychological processes in the development of late-life social identity. In V. W. Marshall (Ed.), *Aging in Canada: Social perspectives* (2nd ed., pp. 60–81). Toronto: Fitzhenry & Whiteside.

Norris, J. E. (1990, October). *Peer relations of the never-married.* Paper presented at the annual meeting of the Canadian Association on Gerontology, Victoria, B.C.

Norris, J. E. (1992). [Friendship in young adulthood.] Unpublished raw data.

Norris, J. E., & Forbes, S. (1987, November). *Cohesion and adap-*

tability in caregiving families. Paper presented at the annual meeting of the Gerontological Society of America, Washington, D.C.

Norris, J. E., & Rubin, K. H. (1984). Peer interaction and communication: A life-span perspective. In P. B. Baltes & O. G. Brim, Jr. (Eds.), *Life-span development and behavior,* Vol. 6. Orlando, Fla.: Academic Press.

Norris, J. E., & Rubin, K. H. (1988, October). *Social contact and well-being in old age.* Paper presented at the annual meeting of the Canadian Association on Gerontology, Halifax, Nova Scotia.

Norris, J. E., & Tari, A. J. (1985). [Grandparenting relations.] Unpublished raw data.

Novak, M. (1993). *Aging and society: A Canadian perspective.* Toronto: Nelson.

Nugent, J. K. (1991). Cultural and psychological influences on the father's role in infant development. *Journal of Marriage and the Family, 53,* 475–485.

O'Bryant, S. L. (1988). Sibling support and older widow's well-being. *Journal of Marriage and the Family, 50,* 173–183.

Ontario Gerontology Association. (1986). *Fact book on aging in Ontario.* Ontario: Author.

Osako, M. (1976). Intergenerational relations as an aspect of assimilation: The case of Japanese Americans. *Sociological Inquiry, 46,* 67–72.

Pagel, M. D., Erdly, W. W., & Becker, J. (1989). Social networks: We get by with (and in spite of) a little help from our friends. *Journal of Personality and Social Psychology, 53,* 793–804.

Palkovitz, R. (1988). Trials and triumphs in the transition to parenthood.

Marriage and Family Review, 12, 1–5.

Peterson, G. W., & Rollins, B. C. (1987). Parent–child socialization. In M. B. Sussman & S. K. Steinmetz (Eds.), *Handbook of marriage and the family* (pp. 471–507). New York: Plenum.

Petrowsky, M. (1976). Marital status, sex and the social networks of the elderly. *Journal of Marriage and the Family, 38*, 749–756.

Pineo, P. (1968). Disenchantment in the later years of marriage. In B. Neugarten (Ed.), *Middle age and aging* (pp. 258–262). Chicago: University of Chicago Press.

Pittman, J. F., & Lloyd, S. A. (1988). Quality of family life, social support, and stress. *Journal of Marriage and the Family, 50*, 53–67.

Pogrebin, L. C. (1987). *Among friends.* New York: McGraw-Hill.

Polit, D. F., & Falbo, T. (1987). Only children and personality development: A quantitative review. *Journal of Marriage and the Family , 49*, 309–325.

Pulakos, J. (1987). Brothers and sisters: Nature and importance of the adult bond. *Journal of Psychology, 121*, 521–522.

Pulakos, J. (1990). Correlations between family environment and relationships of young adult siblings. *Psychological Reports, 67*, 1283–1286.

Radin, N. (1988). Primary caregiving fathers of long duration. In P. Bronstein & C. P. Cowan (Eds.), *Fatherhood today: Men's changing role in the family* (pp. 127–143). New York: John Wiley & Sons.

Radloff, L. S. (1980). Depression and the empty nest. *Sex Roles, 6*, 775–781.

Reisman, J. M. (1981). Adult friendships. In S. Duck & R. Gilmour (Eds.), *Personal relationships, Vol. 2: Developing personal relationships* (pp. 205–230). London: Sage.

Rhyne, D. (1981). Bases of marital satisfaction among men and women. *Journal of Marriage and the Family, 43*, 941–955.

Rice, E. P. (1990). *Intimate relationships, marriages, and families.* Mountain View, Calif.: Mayfield.

Roberto, K. A., & Scott, J. P. (1986). Equity considerations in the friendship of older adults. *Journal of Gerontology, 41*, 241–247.

Roberts, R. E., & Bengtson, V. L. (1990). Is intergenerational solidarity a unidimensional construct? A second test of a formal model. *Journal of Gerontology, 45*, S12–20.

Robertson, J. F. (1975). Interaction in three-generation families, parents as mediators: Toward a theoretical perspective. *International Journal of Aging and Human Development, 6*, 103–110.

Robertson, J. F. (1976). Significance of grandparents—Perceptions of young adult grandchildren. *Gerontologist, 16*, 137–140.

Robertson, J. F. (1977). Grandmotherhood: A study of role conception. *Journal of Marriage and the Family, 33*, 165–174.

Robinson, G. E., & Stacey-Konnert, C. (1992, October). *The effects of cognitive impairment on grandchild/grandparent relationships.* Paper presented at the annual meeting of the Canadian Association on Gerontology, Edmonton, Alberta.

Rogers, L. P., & Markides, K. S. (1989). Well-being in the postparental stage in Mexican–American women. *Research on Aging, 11*, 508–516.

Rook, K. S. (1987). Reciprocity of social exchange and social satisfaction among older women. *Journal of Personality and Social Psychology, 52,* 145–154.

Rose, S. M. (1985). Same- and cross-sex friendships and the psychology of homosociality. *Sex Roles, 12,* 63–74.

Rosenberg, E. B. (1992). *The adoption life cycle: The children and their families through the years.* New York: Free Press.

Rovner, S. (1990, December 28). Good-bye to empty-nest. *Kitchener-Waterloo Record,* p. D1.

Rubin, L. (1985). *Just friends.* New York: Harper & Row.

Sandelowski, M., Harris, B. G., & Holditch-Davis, D. (1991). "The clock is ticking, the calendar pages are turning and we are still waiting": Infertile couples' encounters with time in the adoption waiting period. *Qualitative Sociology, 23,* 143–173.

Sandelowski, M., Holditch-Davis, D., & Harris, B. G. (1990). Living the life: Explanations of infertility. *Sociology of Health and Illness, 12,* 194–215.

Sandelowski, M., Holditch-Davis, D., & Harris, B. G. (1992). Using qualitative and quantitative methods: The transition to parenthood among infertile couples. In J. F. Gilgun, K. Daly, & G. Handel (Eds.), *Qualitative methods in family research* (pp. 301–322). Newbury Park, Calif.: Sage.

Sanders, G. F., & Trygstad, D. W. (1989). Stepgrandparents and grandparents: The view from young adults. *Family Relations, 38,* 71–75.

Santrock, J. W., Sitterle, K. A., & Warshak, R. A. (1988). Parent–child relationships in stepfather families. In P. Bronstein & C. P. Cowan (Eds.), *Fatherhood today: Men's changing role in the family* (pp. 144–165). New York: John Wiley & Sons.

Scanzoni, J. (1979). Social processes and power in families. In W. Burr, R. Hill, F. Nye, & I. Reiss (Eds.), *Contemporary theories about the family, Vol. 1: Research-based theories.* New York: Free Press.

Scharrenbroich, R. (1986). I am an endangered species. In F. M. Burck (Ed.), *Mothers talking: Sharing the secret* (pp. 143–150). New York: St. Martin's Press.

Schnaiberg, A., & Goldenberg, S. (1989). From empty nest to crowded nest: The dynamics of incompletely launched young adults. *Social Problems, 36,* 251–269.

Schumm, W. R., & Bugaighis, M. A. (1986). Marital quality over the marital career: Alternative explanations. *Journal of Marriage and the Family, 48,* 165–168.

Schusky, E. L. (1965). *Manual for kinship analysis.* Chicago: Holt, Rinehart & Winston.

Scott, N. (1992, January 11). Some adult kids welcomed back to the nest. *Kitchener-Waterloo Record,* p. D1.

Seltzer, M. M. (1989). The three r's of life cycle sibships. *American Behavioral Scientist, 33,* 107–115.

Semple, S. J. (1985). *A generational model of child care: Intergenerational attitudes toward child-rearing practices.* Unpublished master's thesis, University of Guelph, Guelph, Ontario.

Settles, B. H. (1987). A perspective on tomorrow's families. In M. B. Sussman & S. K. Steinmetz (Eds.), *Handbook of marriage and the family* (pp. 157–180). New York: Plenum.

Shanas, E., & Sussman, M. (1981). The family in later life: Social structure and social policy. In R. W. Fogel, E.

Hatfield, S. B. Kiesler, & E. Shanas (Eds.), *Aging: Stability and change in the family* (pp. 211–249). New York: Academic Press.

Shaver, P. R., & Hazan, C. (1988). A biased overview of the study of love. *Journal of Social and Personal Relationships, 5*, 473–501.

Spanier, G. B., & Furstenberg, F. F., Jr. (1987). Remarriage and reconstituted families. In M. B. Sussman & S. K. Steinmetz (Eds.), *Handbook of marriage and the family*. New York: Plenum.

Spitze, G., & Logan, J. R. (1992). Helping as a component of parent–adult child relations. *Research on Aging, 14*, 291–312.

Sporakowski, M. J., & Axelson, L. J. (1984). Long-term marriages: A critical review. *Lifestyles: A Journal of Changing Patterns, 7*, 76–93.

Sporakowski, M., & Hughston, G. (1978). Prescriptions for happy marriage: Adjustments and satisfactions of couples married for 50 or more years. *The Family Coordinator, 27*, 321–327.

Steinberg, L., & Silverberg, S. B. (1987). Influences on marital satisfaction during the middle stages of the family life cycle. *Journal of Marriage and the Family, 49*, 751–760.

Stock, C. (1974). *All our kin*. New York: Harper and Row.

Stone, E. (1992, April). Friends again: When sisters become moms. *Parents*, pp. 91–96.

Strain, L. A., & Chappell, N. L. (1982). Confidants: Do they make a difference in quality of life. *Research on Aging, 4*, 479–502.

Suggs, P. K. (1989). Predictors of association among older siblings: A black/white comparison. *American Behavioral Scientist, 33*, 70–79.

Suitor, J. J., & Pillemer, K. (1987). The presence of adult children: A source of stress for elderly couples' marriages? *Journal of Marriage and the Family, 49*, 717–725.

Suitor, J. J., & Pillemer, K. (1988). Explaining intergenerational conflict when adult children and elderly parents live together. *Journal of Marriage and the Family, 50*, 1037–1047.

Sussman, M. (1988). Another perspective on the trials and triumphs in the transition to parenthood. *Marriage and Family Review, 12*, 7–11.

Tari, A. (1983). The extended family revisited: A sociopsychological study. *Pszichologia* (Hungary).

Taylor, R. J., Chatters, L. M., Tucker, M. B., & Lewis, E. (1990). Developments in research on black families: A decade review. *Journal of Marriage and the Family, 52*, 993–1014.

Tennant, P. (1992, March 6). Cut the cord before sharing the house. *Kitchener-Waterloo Record*, p. F1.

Tesch, S. A. (1989). Early-life development and adult friendship. In R. G. Adams & R. Blieszner (Eds.), *Older adult friendship: Structure and process* (pp. 89–107). Newbury Park, Calif.: Sage.

Thomas, J. L. (1990). The grandparent role: A double bind. *International Journal of Aging and Human Development, 31*, 169–177.

Thomlison, R. J., & Foote, C. E. (1991). Children and the law in Canada: The shifting balance of children's, parents', and the state's rights. In J. Veevers (Ed.), *Continuity and change in marriage and family* (pp. 439–449). Toronto: Holt, Rinehart & Winston.

Thompson, L., & Walker, A. J. (1984). Mothers and daughters: Aid patterns and attachment. *Journal of Marriage and the Family, 46,* 313–322.

Tindale, J. A. (1989). [Unemployment and older workers.] Unpublished raw data.

Tindale, J. A. (1991). *Older workers in an aging work force: No. 9, Writings in Gerontology.* Ottawa: National Advisory Council on Aging.

Titus, S. S. (1980). A function of friendship: Social comparisons as a frame of reference for marriage. *Human Relations, 33,* 409–431.

Tomlin, A. M., & Passman, R. H. (1991). Grandmothers' advice about disciplining grandchildren: Is it accepted by mothers, and does rejection influence grandmothers' subsequent guidance? *Psychology and Aging, 6,* 182–189.

Treas, J., & Bengtson, V. (1987). The family in later years. In M. B. Sussman & S. K. Steinmetz (Eds.), *Handbook of marriage and the family,* (pp. 625–648). New York: Plenum.

Troll, L. E. (1975). *Early and middle adulthood.* Monterey, Calif.: Brooks/Cole.

Troll, L. E. (1975). *Early and middle childhood: The best is yet to be . . . maybe.* Pacific Grove, Calif.: Brooks/Cole.

Troll, L. E. (1985). The contingencies of grandparenting. In V. L. Bengtson & J. F. Robertson (Eds.), *Grandparenthood* (pp. 135–149). Beverly Hills, Calif.: Sage.

Troll, L. E., & Smith, J. (1976). Attachment through the life span: Some questions about dyadic bonds among adults. *Human Development, 19,* 156–170.

Tucker, R. D., Marshall, V. W., Longino, C. F. Jr., & Mullins, L. C. (1988). Older Anglophone Canadians in Florida: An historical over-

view. *Canadian Journal on Aging, 7,* 218–232.

Twins born to California grandmother. (1992, November). *Guelph Mercury,* p. 2A.

Ubellacker, S. (1993, February 22). Home is where they have to take you in. *Kitchener-Waterloo Record,* p. D1.

Uhlenberg, P., & Cooney, T. M. (1990). Family size and mother–child relations in later life. *American Behavioral Scientist, 33,* 70–79.

Underwood, N., & DeMont, J. (1991, August 19). Mid-life panic. *Maclean's,* pp. 30–33.

Vachon, M. L. S., & Stylianos, S. K. (1988). The role of social support in bereavement. *Journal of Social Issues, 44,* 175–190.

Veevers, J. E. (1991). *Continuity and change in marriage and the family.* Toronto: Holt, Rinehart & Winston.

Walker, A. J., & Allen, K. R. (1991). Relationships between caregiving daughters and their elderly mothers. *Gerontologist, 31,* 389–396.

Wallace, P. M., & Gotlib, I. H. (1990). Marital adjustment during the transition to parenthood: Stability and predictors of change. *Journal of Marriage and the Family, 52,* 21–29.

Walster, E., Walster, G. W., & Berscheid, E. (1978). *Equity: Theory and research.* Boston: Allyn & Bacon.

Ward, R., Logan, J., & Spitze, G. (1992). The influence of parent and child needs on coresidence in middle and later life. *Journal of Marriage and the Family, 54,* 209–221.

Weihaus, S., & Field, D. (1988). A half century of marriage: Continuity or change? *Journal of Marriage and the Family, 50,* 763–774.

Weisner, T. S., & Gallimore, R. (1977). My brother's keeper: Child and sibling caretaking. *Current Anthropology*, *18*, 169–190.

Weiss, R. S. (1982). Attachment in adult life. In C. M. Parkes & J. Stevenson-Hinde (Eds.), *The place of attachment in human behavior* (pp. 171–184). New York: Basic Books.

Wentowski, G. J. (1981). Reciprocity and the coping strategies of older people: Cultural dimensions of network building. *Gerontologist*, *21*, 600–609.

West, M., Sheldon, A., & Reiffer, L. (1987). An approach to the delineation of adult attachment: Scale development and reliability. *Journal of Nervous and Mental Disease*, *175*, 738–741.

White, L. K., & Booth, A. V. (1985). The transition to parenthood and marital quality. *Journal of Family Issues*, *6*, 435–449.

White, L. K., & Edwards, J. N. (1990). Emptying the nest and parental well-being: An Analysis of national panel data. *American Sociological Review*, *55*, 235–242.

White, L. K., & Riedmann, A. (1992). When the Brady bunch grows up: Step/half- and full-sibling relationships in adulthood. *Journal of Marriage and the Family*, *54*, 197–208.

Wilkinson, D. (1987). Ethnicity. In M. B. Sussman & S. K. Steinmetz (Eds.), *Handbook of marriage and the family* (pp. 183–210). New York: Plenum.

Wilson, M. N. (1989). Child development in the context of the black extended family. *American Psychologist*, *44*, 380–385.

Wiseman, J. P. (1986). Friendship: Bonds and binds in a voluntary relationship. *Journal of Social and Personal Relationships*, *3*, 191–211.

Wister, A. (1985). Living arrangement choices among the elderly. *Canadian Journal on Aging*, *4*, 127–144.

Wright, P. H. (1989). Gender differences in adults' same- and cross-gender friendships. In R. G. Adams & R. Blieszner (Eds.), *Older adult friendship* (pp. 197–221). Newbury Park, Calif.: Sage.

Wright, P. H., & Bergloff, P. J. (1984). *The acquaintance description form and the comparative study of interpersonal relationships*. Paper presented at the Second International Conference on Personal Relationships.

Zube, M. (1982). Changing behavior and outlook of aging men and women: Implications for marriage in the middle and later years. *Family Relations*, *31*, 147–156.

Zwarun, S. (1991, July). Trapped in the sandwich generation. *Chatelaine*, pp. 59–63.

Author Index

Subject Index